KU-407-329

AUDREY GORDON'S
TUSCAN SUMMER

hardie grant books

MELBOURNE · LONDON

AUDREY GORDON'S
TUSCAN SUMMER

RECIPES & RECOLLECTIONS
FROM THE HEART OF ITALY

With Audrey & Phillip Gordon

Audrey Gordon would like to thank:

Heidi Arena, Daniel Atkins, Rina Breda, Michele Burch, Rhiannon Campbell, Tess Clark, Tanya De Silva, Anna and Brad Dunn, Bronwyn Francis, Hwa Goh, Celia Hirsh, Freda Hirsh, Michael Hirsh, Pauline Hirsh, Kerri and Moreno Mazzocco, Leonie Millard, Mary Muirhead, Jackson Orloff, Skye Orloff, Guiseppe Palmieri, Luigi and Teresina Perri, Timothy Perri, Billy Pinnell, Ceri Wood and Dave Rogers, Lina Scalzo, Aurora Shmith, Woody Shmith, Luisa and Phil Simon, Caroline Styles, Mercedes Valero, Wei Wang

Bacash Restaurant, Eat More Fruit, Villa Parma www.villaparma.com.au

Audrey Gordon would especially like to thank her dear friends Santo Cilauro, Tom Gleisner and Rob Sitch without whose editorial input this book might well not exist.

Published in 2010 by Hardie Grant Books in conjunction with Working Dog Productions Pty Ltd

Hardie Grant Books (Australia)
85 High Street
Prahran, Victoria 3181
www.hardiegrant.com.au

Hardie Grant Books (UK)
Second Floor, North Suite
Dudley House
Southampton Street
London WC2E 7HF
www.hardiegrant.co.uk

Project Manager: Tracy O'Shaughnessy
Project Co-ordinator: Pauline Hirsh
Editor: Janet Austin
Designer: Tanya De Silva
Photographer: Hwa Goh
Additional Images: Ian Burch, Santo Cilauro, Tom Gleisner, Pauline Hirsh
Photo Researcher: Gillian Taylor

Photolibrary (pp. 18, 19, 23, 30, 37, 38, 41, 45, 49, 59, 64, 68, 71, 74, 75, 78, 85, 87, 89, 93, 97, 101, 105, 109, 111, 117, 121, 129, 132, 136, 140, 151, 155, 158, 161, 164, 165, 176, 180, 183, 193, 201, 207, 209, 215, 216)
Shutterstock (front cover inset right, back cover and pp. 9, 16-17, 23, 32-33, 33, 34, 39, 48, 52-53, 74, 82, 88, 102, 110, 112-113, 128, 139, 170-171, 186, 198)
iStockphoto (pp. 3, 20, 22, 23, 62, 73, 104, 126, 130, 184, 188)
Stockfood Australia (pp. 28, 55, 57, 146, 173, 187, 189)
Corbis (pp. 7, 20)

Copyright © Working Dog Productions 2010

Cataloguing-in-Publication data is available from the National Library of Australia

ISBN 978 174270 009 0

Colour reproduction by Splitting Image Colour Studio
Printed and bound in China by C&C Offset Printing

All rights reserved. No part of this publication may be reproduced, stored in a retrieval system or transmitted in any form by any means, electronic, mechanical, photocopying, recording or otherwise, without the prior written permission of the publishers and copyright holders.

DEDICATION
EUNICE MAY FROTTLEY
(1923–2004)

Many of the recipes in this book are family heirlooms handed down
to me by my grandmother, who was a simply wonderful cook.
As a young bride, she kept a comprehensive journal of favourite
recipes clipped from magazines, as well as numerous lists she had
compiled, with fascinating headings such as 'Interesting Herbs'
or 'Dazzling Desserts'. She even had a section labelled
'Things to Never Try Again', which contained a recipe for
borage-ginger soup, along with a photograph of the
coal delivery boy.

FOREWORD

This book is not directed at celebrity super chefs or *haute cuisine* high flyers dazzling diners in their Michelin-starred restaurants. It's written for you, the ordinary cook, stuck at home with insufficient bench space and a set of chipped mixing bowls. My fervent hope is that it will inspire you, and give you the confidence to believe that you can be a wonderful cook or, at the very least, an adequate one.

This book is meant as a guide, not a set of strict rules to be deviated from at your peril! There's no need to slavishly follow my every measurement and step. Doesn't a violinist playing Beethoven occasionally add a few notes to the score? Or an aircraft pilot about to take off sometimes skip a pre-flight safety check or two? Of course! And so should you.

I'm a no-nonsense chef. If a recipe calls for squash and I think thinly sliced courgette will work just as well (not to mention add a peppery crunch), then I'll just go ahead and do it. That's what cooking should be about. Going with one's impulses and to hell with the consequences! That said, I've had years of practice and I simply can't be held responsible for any inevitable disappointment that might arise from your attempts at improvisation. If you are a novice in the kitchen, I'd strongly urge you to follow my recipes closely. And, no matter how experienced you might be, please pay careful attention to each instruction. You'd be amazed at the number of people who read 'gently simmer' and then proceed to 'simmer gently', or who think there's no real difference between chopping tomatoes roughly and chopping them coarsely.

Finally, this book is not meant to be a monologue. I want you to imagine I'm there in the kitchen *with* you, helping, guiding, prodding and – only occasionally – rapping your knuckles with the handle of an egg whisk.

Audrey

XXX

At the end of this book I've left a page or two for notes. If you think you've got something to add that hasn't been covered perfectly adequately already, then feel free to defile the book. But I suggest you think twice before doing so.

GRAZIA!

A book like this doesn't happen without a jolly lot of hard work. The following are just a few of the many people I would like to thank, as well as a few who are included for purely contractual reasons.

✦ First and foremost, my darling husband, Phillip. You are the egg in my omelette. Thank you, thank you, thank you!

✦ My wonderful photographer Desiree Coffts – *molto grazia!* What this woman can do with a glazing brush, a bottle of glycerine and some soft light is nothing short of extraordinary.

✦ Fiona Steed for designing the book so beautifully. Even if some of your amazing ideas (such as printing each recipe on edible rice paper) proved a little too visionary for certain publishers to fully appreciate, let alone agree to provide the funds for, they were nothing short of inspirational and I look forward to working together again.

✦ My food stylist Jo French for her invaluable help and eye for detail. Even when we thought everything looked perfect, she was always able to find some fault – and that is a gift.

✦ My creative designer Angela Pryor, who scoured the second-hand shops of Tuscany for authentic tableware and kitchen appliances. The fact that we were able to use so few of the items she secured in our photo shoots is in no way a reflection on the quality of her work.

✦ My commissioning editor, Hugh Creighton, who not only encouraged and carefully guided this book but also put up with my frequent phone calls complaining about the lack of publisher support. Hugh, I never blamed you *personally* for the budgetary constraints that threatened to derail this wonderful project. Yes, I was cross but I now realise that you are just a very small and relatively unimportant cog in the overall book business. So thank you for doing what you could.

✦ Fiona Scarfe and Siobhan Mullens made useful suggestions.

✦ Leslie Reed, less so.

✦ Tamara Feros, my editor, whose attempts to remove anything she deemed 'extraneous' from this book were as persistent as they were misguided. Ta.

Thanks also to my personal assistant, Claire Bayley, who was with me for over seven years and would still be today if she could just display a slightly more flexible and less strident tone when dealing with other people.

And finally, to the people of Tuscany, who welcomed us into their lives with such a generosity of spirit. Every time we ate together they wanted to share their knowledge and passion for food. In the end it's not *your* recipe or *their* recipe, it's one that belongs to anyone with a love of cooking. (That said, all recipes in this book are mine and any attempt to reproduce them without written permission from my publisher will be met with legal action).

Contents

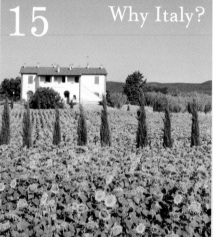

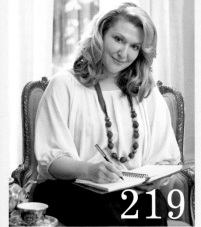

THE RECIPES

I'm not interested in taste from a food-snobbish, status sense (please, I'm just not interested, so stop going on about it!). I am, above all, a practical cook. I realise that the average person doesn't have the time or money to go out and buy a massive list of exotic ingredients and then spend seventeen hours in the kitchen sweating over a pestle while waiting for the lime coulis to reduce.

The recipes in this book are simple, rarely calling for anything more than a few bowls, some saucepans, a set of poultry shears and – on one or two occasions – a nitrogen infuser. What's more, I'm no purist either. If my recipe calls for stock and, instead of slaving for hours over a boiling pot of bones, you want to pick up some shop-bought concentrate – then go right ahead. Provided you can live with this sort of compromise, the decision is entirely yours.

A word on ingredients

There's no need to worry if you can't make it to an authentic Tuscan market! Fortunately, Italy now exports many of its finest products, so anyone can enjoy making these dishes at home. A few specialities, such as lard from Colonnata or sheep's bile from Pienza, cannot be obtained unless you are willing to import the raw ingredients or build your own slaughter pit (see my website for specifications), but most of the recipes in this book consist of easily obtainable items.

While every effort has been made to ensure that the recipes in this book are accurate, I can take no personal responsibility for errors or omissions that may have occurred. I'm *still* getting correspondence related to my last publication which included the instruction to season a dish with 'freshly ground black people'. (Honestly, I sometimes I think readers go out of their way to be offended, don't you?). The fact is, I have *many* dark skinned friends and would never wish to see used to enhance the flavour of foods.

KITCHEN NOTES

Measurements

While there is no shortage of measuring cups, spoons and kitchen scales on the market, I prefer to go by instinct. Pick up a handful of plain organic flour. Does it feel like 10 grams to you? Then it probably is. It's the same with butter and granulated sugar, although slightly less so.

Conversions

The recipes in this book use metric measurements. To convert from metric to imperial, as a general rule, halve the amount and add 1 egg.

Dry

1 cup = 2.4 handfuls

A smattering = 3 scatterings

A smidgen = ½ a blob

Wet

1 glug = 2½ nips

A splash = ½ a splodge

Serving sizes

Each recipe in this book is designed to serve four people. If you are cooking for big eaters (or Americans), you might consider doubling the amounts.

A word on knives

It is absolutely essential that you use the correct knife for the job. A vegetable knife should not be used for paring, any more than you'd cut bread with a carving knife. You don't see a surgeon removing someone's appendix with a meat cleaver, do you? (Although I have heard some absolute horror stories about public hospitals!) It's the same when deflorating artichokes. I find it absolutely heartbreaking to witness an otherwise promising meal being *ruined* during the preparatory stages by carelessly chosen cutting implements. Know your knives. Sharpen them. Love them.

Food hygiene

Hands are the most common way of carrying bacteria from one food to another. When running my restaurants, I always made it a rule to wash my hands with an anti-bacterial cleanser, especially after touching the waste bin or any of the casual staff.

A word on organic ingredients

Throughout this book I advocate the use, where possible, of organic ingredients. Not only do they have more flavour, but food grown organically is so much better for the environment. Yes, I know it might be a little more expensive but when it comes to the future of our planet, it's a small price to pay. And to be honest, I find that food often tastes better when you've paid that little bit more for it, don't you?

SHUTTING UP SHOP

I am, officially, exhausted. It's hard to believe that my husband, Phillip, and I have been running our award-winning restaurant now for almost eleven years, originally as Audrey's (with moderate success) before making the change to audrey's, at which point there was no holding us back!

These past twelve months, in particular, have been somewhat trying. Managing the business, shooting the pilot for my new television series, book signings, countless meetings and public appearances – it was a schedule neither of us could maintain for much longer. Things got so hectic around Christmas that Phillip and I even found ourselves having to prearrange times to make love! Not exactly the most spontaneous or romantic situation, especially when – due to last-minute complications – one of us was often not able to be there.

We closed the door on audrey's on 24 April, reopening it the following day to let the couple at table 17 out, before closing again for good. I can tell you now, shutting the restaurant was not easy. In fact, it was almost like a death in the family – only no one was fighting over the sideboard. The hardest thing was telling our staff, many of whom had been with us for more than a decade. All I can say is thank God for emails – I simply couldn't have faced looking into their eyes.

That said, I feel I've walked away at a good time. I'm proud of what we've achieved over the past decade. Yes, there have been the awards, too many to mention here (you can visit my website for a complete list). And the accolades. Simon Hadwell of the *Guardian* once described our 64-course degustation menu as 'a must-eat event for serious foodies'. But it's more about what we've contributed to the world of food. While I don't take sole credit for putting *vino cotto* back onto the international culinary landscape, there's no doubt our pioneering use of this long-overlooked ingredient has greatly helped restore its rightful place. (I have to laugh at the number of so-called 'cutting edge' establishments that have since blindly aped this trend, thinking no one will remember who actually started it!)

More than all of this, however, what I'm most proud of is the way audrey's made high-quality, innovative cuisine accessible to everyone. Naturally, we had our core clientele of discerning diners, but Phillip and I always made a point of encouraging *ordinary* people to eat at our restaurant. Obviously not on weekends, and we tended to seat them towards the back, but they were most definitely allowed in.

The other motivating factor for closing was the sense that, in many ways, there was nothing more to be achieved. When you've taken out *Table* magazine's 'Best Inner City Ambience' gong three years running, where do you go? I am passionate about food, and will throw myself into any aspect of its promotion, whether cooking for a restaurant full of hungry diners, hosting a Master Class or simply endorsing a new range of fragrant bin liners. But I didn't want to ever reach the stage where this passion began to fade.

I'll be honest, there were a few times when I came perilously close to feeling a sense of ennui. I can clearly remember one wet Wednesday afternoon when I'd rushed across town for a corporate product launch, arriving cold and exhausted. I was in the middle of demonstrating a twin-drawer Dishlex to a group of kitchenware distributors from Luton when I suddenly had a near mental meltdown. I can recall thinking, 'What's the point?' Back home later that night, I told Phillip my worries. Stepping out of the shower, I said to him, 'I think I might be losing my love of food.' The darling took one look at me naked and dripping wet on the bath-mat and replied, 'I can promise you that hasn't happened.' Still, it was a close shave – and clearly time for a change.

That's when the two of us got talking. What if we took a break? Packed everything up and headed someplace where the pace of life was a little slower. Phillip has vivid memories of travelling through France during his gap year, and his eyes lit up as he spoke of the narrow streets, historic chateaux and, of course, the women with their elegant clothes and stylish good looks. Which is why I decided on Italy, or Tuscany to be more precise.

The trip would be a chance for us to step out of the limelight, to get away from the pressures of public life and enjoy a quiet, private break together. And then write a book about it.

We spoke to a few friends about the idea of 'disappearing' for a few months and they were all surprisingly supportive. In fact, before we knew it we found ourselves the guests of honour at a lavish going away party organised by our dear chums Claire and Martin Loveshaw. It was a truly special night, in no way diminished by their uninspired choice of finger food (mini quiches anyone?), and we received some wonderful going away gifts.

Naturally, we told everyone to make sure they came to visit, although Phillip was suitably selective when handing out our actual address (most people just got a post office box). Then, with a final '*arrivederci*' toast, we were on our way.

'Do you ever have one of those days when you simply don't feel like cooking, and even the thought of getting out the frying pan seems all too much? I don't.'

WHY ITALY?

I love Italy. For hundreds of years, if not centuries, the people of Italy (Italians) have been living here. And without doubt the culinary heart of this amazing country would have to be Tuscany. Some of the world's finest olive oil, wines, smallgoods and cheeses come from this fertile region abutting the Ligurian Sea.

In addition to food, there's also the culture of Italy to embrace. This is the land of artists: Michelangelo, Botticelli, Mussolini, not to mention Leonardo da Vinci and my very own 'old master' Phillip. Our trip would give him the chance to pursue his art, something that's had to take a back seat while we ran the restaurant. Phillip's a terribly gifted painter and there couldn't be a better place than Tuscany for him to exercise his muse.

GETTING AWAY

Of course, getting away proved more difficult than we first thought. We had to reassure nervous colleagues that we were only a phone call away, tie up various business deals and organise somewhere to stay. Then there was the packing up at home! As our house-minding service was not able to start for several weeks, we decided to leave the rabbits locked in the laundry with plenty of water and lettuce. We took a similar approach with Phillip's mother.

Much of our luggage was sent on ahead but we still found ourselves at Gatwick in mid-May with some rather over-sized suitcases. I usually find the staff at the check-in counter pretty understanding but wouldn't you know it, we got the employee from hell (or, to be more accurate, Hyderabad). I'm not sure if young Sanjeet was deliberately trying to make life difficult, but frankly I found the concept of someone of her background penalising me for taking too much out of *my own country* just a little hard to take.

Several hours (not to mention gin and tonics!) later, Phillip and I touched down at Fiumicino, collected our hire car – a rather sporty Fiat (when in Rome…!) – and set off, with Phillip behind the wheel and me beside him as navigator.

The road signs were terribly confusing and my last-minute cries of 'left' and 'right' meant that poor Phillip was changing lanes like a modern-day Fangio, much to the annoyance of other drivers. After about half an hour we realised we were lost. Worse, we were still in the airport car park.

Maggio

may

18 May   I can tell you, it was an enormous relief when we reached our hotel, the stylish Piazza Pallazzio, and we wasted no time in depositing our bags and heading out to explore. It had been almost three hours since either of us had eaten (apart from a few packets of crisps in the car), so food was very much priority *numero uno*. And where else to enjoy our first meal but at one of Rome's signature restaurants, Gilberto's. By the time we arrived, the place was pretty full, as was Gilberto himself, a larger-than-life character who – despite success and fame – still makes a habit of personally greeting his patrons. Now that's service!

After a quick *aperitif* at the bar, Phillip and I were seated. I wasted no time in ordering that most quintessential of Roman dishes, oxtail stew. As the steaming plate was placed before me, I knew that, at last, we had arrived!

The Piazza Pallazzio has genuine period charm. Each of its 66 rooms boasts antiques such as Etruscan rugs, four-poster beds, vases and dial-up internet.

Funny, isn't it, how inconsiderate people can be? When it's obvious one is about to take a photo they still insist on wandering into shot!

CODA ALLA VACCINARA
OXTAIL STEW

Many people are put off cooking with cheaper cuts of meat, for the simple reason that they are, well, cheap. Back home, I've found a wonderful butcher who sells oxtail, stewing steak and even chops, all at significantly marked-up prices, so one can shop with peace of mind.

2.5 KG OXTAIL, CUT INTO 20 × 5 CM PIECES

SALT

FRESHLY GROUND BLACK PEPPER

PLAIN FLOUR

125 ML EXTRA-VIRGIN OLIVE OIL

120 G PANCETTA, DICED

3 CLOVES GARLIC, MINCED

3 SMALL ONIONS, HALVED

500 ML DRY WHITE WINE

2 × 400 G CANS ITALIAN TOMATOES,
   JUICES RETAINED

12 STICKS CELERY, CUT INTO 6 CM LENGTHS, OR
   6 STICKS CELERY, CUT INTO 12 CM LENGTHS

2 TABLESPOONS PINE NUTS, TOASTED

2 TABLESPOONS SULTANAS

1. Preheat oven to 180°C.

2. Season the oxtail and dredge it in flour. Pat with your hands so only a dusting of flour remains on the meat.

3. In a large casserole with a lid, heat the olive oil and fry the pancetta until golden brown. Remove with a slotted spoon and reserve.

4. Brown the oxtail thoroughly on all sides in the pancetta oil. Do *not* crowd the oxtail or allow the pieces to touch during this process. This is terribly important and I find it truly upsetting the way some people are willing to compromise the outcome of a dish in the interests of saving a few minutes. Crowded meat will not brown, it will broil, producing a vastly inferior taste. So please think ahead and, if necessary, fry your oxtail in batches or even separate pans to ensure no inadvertent meat mingling.

5. Return all the oxtail to the pan. Insert minced garlic into three of the onion halves, using a spice applicator if you have one (I simply couldn't live without mine!), then add to the pan along with the remaining onion halves and reserved pancetta. Reheat until sizzling.

6. Add the wine and reduce until nearly evaporated. Add the tomatoes, cover with a lid and bake for approximately 4 hours (just long enough to run a decent bath if you're expecting guests and need to freshen up before they arrive), until the meat is very tender.

7. Add the celery to the casserole, ensuring it is covered in sauce, and bake for a further 20 minutes (this is perhaps a good opportunity to dry your hair). Add the pine nuts and sultanas. Continue baking for about 10 minutes (nails?) until the celery is tender.

8. Adjust the seasoning and serve in a cheerful bowl.

AUDREY'S TIP

When pan-frying meat, the trick is to cook it undisturbed in a really hot pan. Don't be tempted to poke and prod it every few seconds. Leave it alone, lower the lights if necessary and keep noise to a minimum. If you live on a particularly busy road, consider having the traffic diverted.

19 May

Whether it was the wonderful Italian light or the sound of someone using the lavatory next door, Phillip and I both woke early. With only one full day in Rome, there was simply too much to explore for either of us to be lazing in bed. After a light breakfast of toast, omelette, fruit and some heavenly Italian pastries washed down with a jug of rich, dark coffee, it was time to head forth.

In terms of attractions, Rome is so overwhelming that we decided to get our bearings by joining a walking tour of the central district. Starting from the earliest Roman days, our guide took us through the many architectural and artistic highlights of this extraordinary city. Cathedrals, fountains, beautifully restored palaces. About forty minutes into the tour, Phillip spotted a delightful café called Struzzi that we had been strongly recommended to visit. Doing so meant missing part of the Renaissance and the Baroque period, but one bite of their freshly baked *biscotti* convinced us it was more than worth it.

Rome truly is an amazing experience, a combination of extraordinary history, culture and style. From our sidewalk café table we watched as a group of fashionably dressed young women clattered past in their stilettos. They turned out to be nuns. Meanwhile, darkly handsome young men sat at the bar drinking Campari, their cardigans draped casually around their necks (a sure sign, Phillip assured me, that they were gay).

All over Rome you see old women standing in doorways wearing black. For many it is because their husbands have died. Others simply consider it slimming.

During the twelfth century Moorish invaders constructed this magnificent palace. Commissioned for Emperor El-Hamani, it took over 40 years to build – although much of this time was apparently spent waiting for the bricks to arrive. The Emperor had his own harem of imperial concubines, who were housed in the most secure section of the palace. It was here that these women, said to be among the most beautiful in the world, would learn the art of pleasing a man by being taught how to dance, sing, recite poetry and correctly re-fold a map.

'Italian cooking is me.
Fresh, vital, changing with the seasons
and faintly redolent of garlic.'

THE VATICAN CITY
The smallest independent nation in the world. Despite being a wealthy, powerful elective monarchy, it's yet to be granted entry into the Eurovision song contest.

Unfortunately, our choice of lunch venue proved less successful. While highly regarded, Ristorante Piccardi turned out to be little more than an overpriced tourist trap. The menu was unimaginative and the service brusque. Our 'Roman' waiter actually turned out to be Romanian, and clearly knew nothing about Italian cuisine. Simply unforgivable in my book, especially when you consider the prices being charged.

Of course, we weren't going to let one bad meal spoil the day and we spent a most enjoyable afternoon exploring some of Rome's most iconic attractions. This time we enlisted the services of a personal guide, Silvio, who proved to be very informative, if a little overly familiar (I'm not sure we needed to hear every detail of his wife's dental problems). But this aside, his knowledge of local architecture and history was most impressive.

One small quibble: I was taken aback by the number of English-speaking tourists who felt entitled to sidle up next to us and listen in on Silvio's commentary. This, to me, is akin to theft, stealing information that we have paid to hear. Naturally, we didn't say anything although Phillip did fix a few of the more pushier interlopers with an icy stare. Some people have no manners.

Our visit to the famous Vatican was marred by lengthy queues that stretched for several hundred metres. To make matters worse, the officials in charge seemed to be employing a rather questionable form of entry criteria, with attractive young women being ushered in ahead of others standing in line. You would expect higher standards, especially from priests, but there you go.

ROME'S FAMOUS COLOSSEUM
Here, fearsome gladiators would fight, often to the death, or at the very least till lunchtime, in front of the enthusiastic crowds. Gladiatorial contests followed a set pattern, beginning with an elaborate procession, led by the sponsor, usually a high-ranking magistrate or local brewer. There would then be preliminary bouts, featuring men fighting exotic wild animals such as lions and tigers, as well as native goats and boars, in order to satisfy local content rules.

THE TREVI FOUNTAIN
Rome's famous fountain attracts thousands of visitors who are all encouraged to toss in a coin, in the belief that those who do so will return to Rome one day. For those without loose change, a credit card facility has recently been installed.

Petty theft is a problem here in Rome and we were advised not to leave the parked car without hiring a young local to keep an eye on it, as well as another older lad to keep an eye on the first.

After struggling to hail a taxi for over half an hour, Phillip and I realised we had no choice but to walk back to the hotel through a maze of crowded streets, full of in-your-face vendors, gangs of gypsy kids and assorted shady characters. Not to mention scores of homeless beggars, wandering about in their filthy rags. As it turned out, many of them were Australian backpackers, but the sense of poverty lying beneath Rome's gilded surface was disturbing.

Phillip wanted to give money to an old woman sitting outside our hotel (she showed him one of her wizened breasts and the poor darling said he felt somewhat obliged), but I assured him that handing out cash to vagrants was not actually helping them. Yes, it might provide food and temporary shelter, but what about a sense of dignity? Besides, as I reminded Phillip, we are already doing more than our fair share back home on the charitable front. I'm a founding member of Chef Aid, a wonderful organisation that arranges for disused kitchen equipment to be sent to underprivileged countries. Just last month we shipped 200 grape scissors to a remote village in northern India, while somewhere in the Sudan there's a subsistence farming community who, thanks to us, are now the proud owners of a rotary evaporator. So, when it comes to doing our bit for others, I think we can both rest pretty comfortably.

Here's a quintessentially Roman sight: a tripe shop. Tripe, or trippa *in Italian, is the lining of the stomach of ruminants such as cows, oxen, sheep and deer. Technically, giraffes also qualify, but this variety is less common and considerably more expensive. (It also needs to be ordered well in advance.)*

'Wouldn't the world be a better place if we could rid it of poverty and prejudice, along with pre-grated parmesan cheese and over-filled wine glasses…?'

20 May After a light breakfast of toast and fresh fruit, washed down with a steaming cup of *caffé latte*, it was time to bid farewell to the Piazza Pallazzio and head north. Our wonderful hosts, Salvatore and Marissa, were genuinely sad to see us go, kissing us on both cheeks as we left the foyer and asking about our plans for the rest of the trip. Just as we managed to reach the door, Salvatore said he 'had something special for us', and pressed a small envelope into Phillip's hands. '*Una memoria,*' he explained. It turned out to be a bill for late check-out.

Finding our way out of Rome and onto the *autostrada* proved something of a challenge, despite our car being fitted with a satellite navigation system. Phillip could not work out how to set it on English; the best he could do was German, and consequently much of the journey was spent listening to a rather peremptory voice shouting *schnell!* every time we missed a turn-off or pulled over for a rest stop.

After a few hours we had left Roma behind and were well on our way. To be honest, it was hard to tell exactly where we were as the view from the *autostrada* was largely made up of truck stops and billboards. We only realised that we had entered the fabled foothills of Tuscany when the tollway tickets changed colour.

I had made sure to pack a few snacks for the trip, some *grissini* and freshly baked *Amaretti* biscuits, but by the time we reached our destination, the village of San Cisterno, both of us were very nearly famished. It was with great relief that we pulled into the driveway of Villa del Vecchio, our home for the coming months.

VILLA DEL VECCHIO

Like many people, we had been dreaming about buying a villa in Tuscany for quite a few years. Just a little place we could get away to over summer. But there simply weren't many suitable places on the market, and those that were for sale came with ridiculous price tags. Then we heard about a splendid little villa in the township of San Cisterno, about half an hour's drive from Siena, that seemed to meet our requirements. Of course, the owners wanted far too much for it and we were about to walk away when we had a stroke of luck, quite literally – one of the owners had a massive cerebral haemorrhage and they were forced to hurriedly sell. Knowing they were desperate, Phillip and I wasted no time putting in an offer (well below the asking price) and a few weeks later the place was ours!

The house itself is exquisite. As is typical of the village, it's made of stone and heavy wooden beams, topped by a high gable of terracotta tiles. From the front you could easily imagine yourself stepping into an original eighteenth-century farmhouse, were it not for the satellite dish and security cameras protruding from the roof.

After such a long trip, it was wonderful to have our neighbours Paolo and Mariella Pasquini waiting at the house to greet us when we arrived. Signora Pasquini came over to us, smiling broadly and wiping her hands on a bloodied apron. Without a moment's hesitation, she planted a kiss on each of our cheeks. Paolo was no less effusive when he joined us, shaking Phillip's hand warmly as if greeting a long-lost friend.

In no time we were all sitting around the wooden table in the huge kitchen of Villa del Vecchio, drinking wine and chatting away in a mangled mix of English and Italian. Before leaving, Paolo and Mariella presented us with a wonderful 'welcome basket' made up of olive oil from Signor Pasquini's own trees, along with cheese, bread and some rather detailed holy cards featuring a local saint being eviscerated with what appeared to be a garden fork.

POLLO ALLA TOSCANA
TUSCAN CHICKEN

In honour of our first night at Villa del Vecchio, I decided to cook this classic
Tuscan dish. Served with a crisp green salad and some bread to mop up the juices,
it's a perfect meal to enjoy outdoors on a warm summer's night, something we almost
certainly would have done had it not been raining steadily. Phillip tried stringing some
plastic sheeting over the terrace but it kept blowing off so in the end we were forced
to abandon our *al fresco* supper and retreat indoors. Still, nothing could 'dampen'
our enjoyment of this flavoursome feast.

1. Preheat oven and a roasting tray to 220°C. Wash the chicken inside
   and out and pat dry with kitchen towel.

2. Using your fingers, separate the skin from the breast meat, being
   careful not to rip the skin. Slice the lemon and work the slices under
   the skin over each breast. Smooth the skin back in place and wipe
   the chicken dry.

3. Rub 2 tablespoons of olive oil seasoned with salt and pepper over
   the bird. Really massage it in, paying particular attention to the
   back, shoulders and other common areas of tension.

4. Push the prosciutto, garlic and thyme into the cavity and put your
   chicken on the hot roasting tray to cook for 20 minutes.

5. While the chicken is cooking, parboil the potatoes in salted water
   for 10 minutes and drain. Add the potatoes to the tray and continue
   to roast for 40 minutes. Reduce oven temperature to 200°C and
   cook for a further 15 minutes.

6. To tell whether the chicken is done, insert a fine skewer into one of
   the thighs. If the juices run clear, then it's ready to eat. If you detect
   blood, either the chicken is under-cooked or you've stabbed yourself.

7. Remove the chicken to a heated platter and cover loosely with
   foil. The potatoes may require a further 10 minutes in the oven
   for crisping.

I × 900 G CHICKEN, PREFERABLY CORN-FED

I LARGE LEMON

60 ML EXTRA-VIRGIN OLIVE OIL

SALT

FRESHLY GROUND BLACK PEPPER

8 SLICES PROSCIUTTO, THINLY SLICED

2 CLOVES GARLIC, FINELY CHOPPED

2 GOOD HANDFULS FRESH THYME LEAVES,
   COARSELY CHOPPED

4 LARGE POTATOES, QUARTERED

AUDREY'S TIP

If you can't find proper prosciutto at your local shops, you
can use ordinary bacon or perhaps consider moving to a
better suburb.

21 May

Not surprisingly, we slept in late this morning, only woken by the sound of Mariella bringing over some freshly picked courgettes.

There's nothing like having good neighbours, and we've been blessed with two wonderful people. Signor and Signora Pasquini have lived in San Cisterno their entire lives and have both proved a font of wisdom and local knowledge. Walking through the village with Mariella this morning, she was able to point out everything from where to find wild herbs to which shops sell the best cheese. Her ability to point out which young girls have recently had an abortion was equally impressive, if of somewhat less practical value.

Meanwhile, back at the villa, when Phillip was struggling to get the old wood stove burning properly, Paolo was able to show him the correct way of adjusting the flue, joking as he did so that 'only a local is smart enough' to operate such things.

They've both been so welcoming and helpful that the least we could do was invite them for dinner tonight. Paolo brought a bottle of homemade *grappa*, while Mariella provided grace, an impassioned prayer that went on for so long I seriously thought I might have to reheat the entrée.

The Pasquinis – our new neighbours.

FIORI DI ZUCCHINI
COURGETTE FLOWERS

Deep-fried courgette flowers were a common sight on Italian restaurant menus in the 1990s, which is the very reason we stopped serving them. But they have since made a comeback and are very popular here in Tuscany as a first course. One of the things I love is that you can use a wide variety of stuffings: finely chopped *bocconcini*, diced *mortadella* sausage, salty *ricotta* or indeed anything – provided it is fresh and in *italics*.

¾ CUP PLAIN FLOUR

80 ML EXTRA-VIRGIN OLIVE OIL,
    PLUS EXTRA FOR FRYING

SALT

250 ML WATER (PREFERABLY SAN PELLEGRINO)

2 EGG WHITES

12 COURGETTE FLOWERS

1. To make the batter, combine the flour, olive oil, salt and water (but not necessarily in that order). Work until smooth then leave to rest for an hour.

2. Beat the egg whites until stiff and compliant, then fold into the batter.

3. Pour olive oil into a large saucepan to a depth of 3 cm and heat. The oil will be hot enough when a small drop of batter dropped into it browns immediately.*

4. Dip the courgette flowers into the batter and fry on both sides until golden brown.

5. Drain well on kitchen towel and serve immediately, sprinkled with salt.

AUDREY'S TIP

* There are several other ways to check the temperature of your oil. The most obvious is with a thermometer, but you can also use the handle of a wooden spoon by dipping it in and seeing if the oil bubbles. Back in my *sous* chef days, the most common method was to flick hot oil at one of the newer kitchenhands and see how loudly they yelled. Thankfully, this practice has been abandoned, as it was not only cruel but also quite inaccurate.

22 May Well, it's been an exciting if somewhat eventful start to proceedings here at Casa Gordon! No sooner had we got all the bags unpacked this morning when the hot water system decided to stop working. Naturally, it was yours truly who was in the shower at the time, with a head covered in rather expensive shampoo.

A few frantic calls later we'd secured the services of Signor Giancarlo Limbardi, the local plumber, who arrived soon after in a charming old car, belching noxious fumes. After casting a cursory eye over the hot water unit, he proceeded to light a small gas stove and began brewing a coffee. Eventually, he got around to inspecting the building's plumbing, at which point he emerged from under the house, crossed himself twice and declared, '*No problema.*' 'Yes, but can you fix it?' I asked. '*No problema!*' replied the doughty tradesman. With a bit of luck, we'll have hot water by the weekend.

This afternoon Phillip and I walked into town to buy a few provisions and generally have a look around. I would have to say that Italians are the friendliest people in the world. We've only been here two days but already we're being treated like locals. As we walk through town, people smile and call '*Buongiorno*' or '*Come sta?*' When we answer, '*Molto bene, grazie,*' they are truly delighted, clapping their hands and launching into an animated exchange, at which point they realise these are the only three words we know, and tend to shuffle off.

Villa del Vecchio, our Italian home. If you ask me, there's no better way to understand a people than by living with them, sharing their food and buying their real estate.

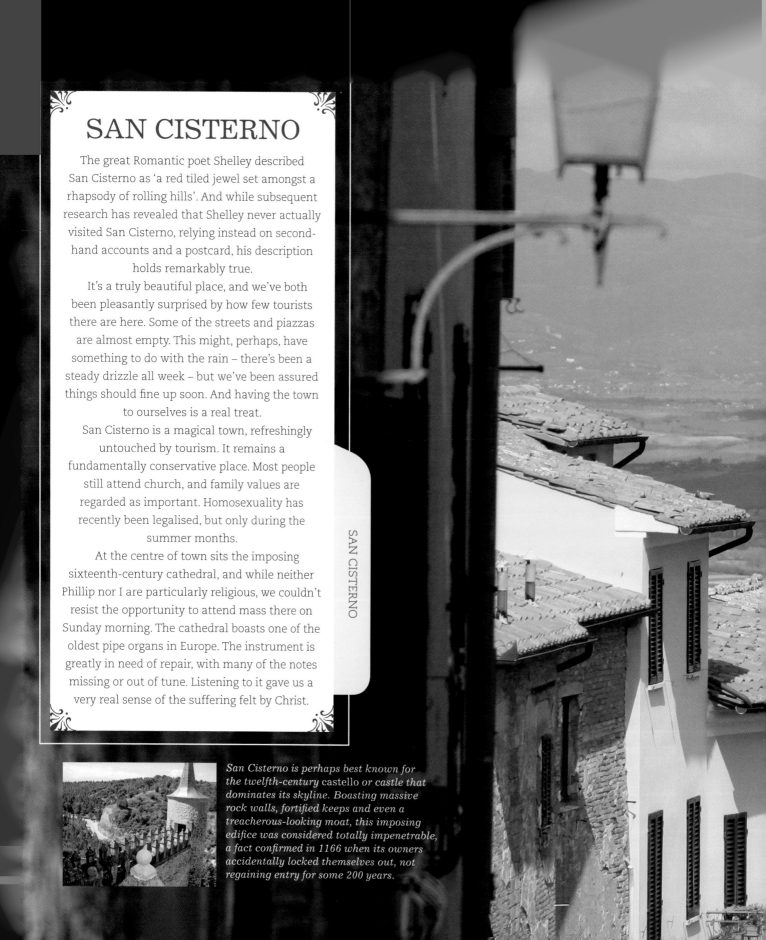

SAN CISTERNO

The great Romantic poet Shelley described San Cisterno as 'a red tiled jewel set amongst a rhapsody of rolling hills'. And while subsequent research has revealed that Shelley never actually visited San Cisterno, relying instead on second-hand accounts and a postcard, his description holds remarkably true.

It's a truly beautiful place, and we've both been pleasantly surprised by how few tourists there are here. Some of the streets and piazzas are almost empty. This might, perhaps, have something to do with the rain – there's been a steady drizzle all week – but we've been assured things should fine up soon. And having the town to ourselves is a real treat.

San Cisterno is a magical town, refreshingly untouched by tourism. It remains a fundamentally conservative place. Most people still attend church, and family values are regarded as important. Homosexuality has recently been legalised, but only during the summer months.

At the centre of town sits the imposing sixteenth-century cathedral, and while neither Phillip nor I are particularly religious, we couldn't resist the opportunity to attend mass there on Sunday morning. The cathedral boasts one of the oldest pipe organs in Europe. The instrument is greatly in need of repair, with many of the notes missing or out of tune. Listening to it gave us a very real sense of the suffering felt by Christ.

San Cisterno is perhaps best known for the twelfth-century castello or castle that dominates its skyline. Boasting massive rock walls, fortified keeps and even a treacherous-looking moat, this imposing edifice was considered totally impenetrable, a fact confirmed in 1166 when its owners accidentally locked themselves out, not regaining entry for some 200 years.

SAN CISTERNO CATHEDRAL
The cathedral is home to a chalice that many claim was used by Christ during the Last Supper, a belief they refuse to give up despite recent tests revealing it is made from 70 per cent aluminium.

[ABOVE] In one corner of the church confessions are heard by a priest, as well as anyone interested enough to sit nearby.

It's not known for sure who was responsible for the first permanent structures in San Cisterno. Certainly, by 100BC numerous tribes were dwelling on the site of the present-day city. Around this time various primitive stone shelters were constructed, most of which have long since collapsed, or been turned into backpacker accommodation.

QUINTUS METELLUS
The first permanent settlement in San Cisterno was established by Roman consul Quintus Metellus, who arrived here in 123 BC. According to legend, Metellus was crossing the boggy plains when his horse became trapped in mud and many of his battalion contracted pneumonia, prompting Quintus to declare, 'This is the place for a town.' Despite later insisting that he was 'merely being sarcastic', a military outpost was established.

Scientists long assumed that the area around San Cisterno was uninhabited in ancient times. That was until only a few years ago when a bone was discovered, belonging to a Neolithic woman. This came as an enormous surprise, not only to archaeologists, but also to the restaurant patron in whose zuppa di giorno the skeletal artefact was found floating.

23 May

Plumbing problems aside, it hasn't taken long for us both to settle in here. Within the space of a few days, we have completely forgotten the cold and dreariness of England, throwing ourselves with gusto into life at Villa del Vecchio.

Phillip already has his paints out and is looking forward to being inspired by the local landscape, once the misty rain lifts long enough for him to catch a decent glimpse of it. An unusually wet spring has seen steady rain linger on but, you know what? We've barely noticed it in all the excitement of settling in. Many of the shops here are still shut for the off-season but we've been assured it's only a matter of time before they're all open for business.

I'm so thrilled to see Phillip painting again, especially after the disappointment of last year when his exhibition was forced to close prematurely. Of course, the gallery made all sorts of pitiful excuses but in the end the small number of people attending could only be blamed on one thing and that's poor advertising. What other explanation could there possibly be? But such events are all in the past and Phillip is now talking excitedly about the possibility of a new exhibition. Watch out, art world!

Luda, the Pasquinis' striking granddaughter. From the moment she appeared, I could tell Phillip was keen to get her down on canvas.

My modern day Caravaggio hard at work.

'I've always loved animals and as a child I collected many pets: everything from stray dogs to turtles and geese. These creatures quickly became my companions and, in some cases, my earliest ingredients.'

24 May

Despite a continuing lack of hot water, I've been busily experimenting in the kitchen and, with no phones or emails to disturb us, it's pure bliss! Honestly, who needs all the distracting mod-cons of twenty-first-century living? I could so easily embrace the life of a Tuscan *contadino*, sleeping rough on a bed of straw and surviving on a few nuts or berries. Of course, I'd need my goose-down pillow and a proper cup of Earl Grey each morning, but apart from that, I could truly live like a peasant.

The more I learn about it, the more I realise that the food here is, above all, about simplicity. Many Tuscans can still remember a time when the day's main meal was little more than *pane e companatico* – 'bread and something to go with the bread' (quite often more bread). It is a cuisine born out of poverty.

Fortunately, living standards have since risen and 80 per cent of locals now own their own homes (while 75 per cent own their own teeth), but frugality lives on in recipes such as nettle soup or dried bean casserole. Little is ever thrown away in a Tuscan kitchen. Stale bread, old bones, vegetable peelings, even used dishcloths will find their way into a typical meal. And, for many, that meal will be *ribollita*…

RIBOLLITA
RIBOLLITA

A staple part of the diet for many Tuscan farmers, this almost clear vegetable broth was traditionally eaten with a fork, perhaps explaining the high rate of malnutrition among the rural community. To fill it out, stale bread is often added. Don't worry if you haven't got any stale bread; many speciality food shops now stock pre-aged pastry products.

2 1/8 CUPS DRIED WHITE CANNELLINI BEANS

200 ML OLIVE OIL

2 CLOVES GARLIC, CHOPPED

100 G WHITE ONIONS, CHOPPED

300 G CARROTS, CHOPPED

300 G CELERY, ROUGHLY CHOPPED

SALT

FRESHLY GROUND BLACK PEPPER

400 G COURGETTES, MANHANDLED

1 LITRE VEGETABLE STOCK

100 G TOMATOES, PEELED AND PULPED.
  THEN LEFT TO THINK ABOUT IT

200 G SPINACH, LIGHTLY CASTIGATED

PARSLEY, TO GARNISH

1. Place the cannellini beans in a large pot, cover with water and bring slowly to the boil. Cook on a very low heat for about 3 weeks, until tender.

2. Heat the olive oil in a large pan and add the garlic and onions. Cook gently until the onions are soft and unsuspecting.

3. Splodge in the carrots and celery, season with salt and pepper and cook over a low heat for 15 minutes.

4. Add the courgettes and leave to sweat for about 10 minutes, then add the beans, stock and tomatoes. Simmer, covered, for 30 minutes.

5. Skim regularly with a slotted spoon to remove any scum (this can be discarded, or used to make *Scum risotto*).

6. Stir in the spinach just before serving and garnish with parsley.

AUDREY'S TIP

Ribollita is traditionally served at the table from a large bowl. This beautiful tureen once belonged to my grandmother, who used it during her later years as a chamber pot.

25 May

We thought the rain was beginning to ease off but unfortunately it looks like it's set in for the week. This is not a problem as I've been busying myself getting the house organised and the kitchen set up.

During breaks in the weather we've made several trips into town to stock up on provisions, and I'm thoroughly enjoying getting to know the various market stallholders. Honestly, I can't *imagine* shopping anywhere else.

Here, the concept of something being 'in season' is taken very seriously, and you never know what will be on offer each day. Put simply, if it's not ripe, it's not sold. This means having to develop a certain flexibility when planning your meals. If, for example, I was thinking of cooking roasted capsicums with a basil and artichoke purée, but the artichokes were not available, I would have to make the dish with, say, grilled aubergines or perhaps shaved fennel. Naturally, this sort of last-minute improvisation can lead to some fairly 'white knuckle' moments in the kitchen but really, I wouldn't have it any other way!

I simply love the vitality of these gregarious, garrulous people. At home in England, we tend to pass each other in the street unnoticed, head down, in a hurry or – worse – plugged into some infernal music machine. Here, not a person goes by without stopping to exchange greetings and share bad news. In a surprisingly large number of instances, this news seems to centre on recent physical ailments, but at least it's communicating.

ABOUT TUSCAN COOKING

The origins of Tuscan cooking date back almost three thousand years to when the region was settled by the Etruscans. Their tombs contain beautiful frescoes showing, among other things, *parpardelle* (noodles), colanders, cheese graters and even a protective cloth emblazoned with images of a woman's breasts – believed to be one of the oldest novelty BBQ aprons yet found. Other frescoes show Etruscan diners reclining elegantly, plates and wine goblets in hand, while waiters hover nearby holding oversized pepper grinders.

There is no such thing as 'Italian' food. It's totally regional: from Naples, Venice, Sicily, etc. In fact, I'll go further and say it's based on individual *villages*, with each small town convinced that theirs is the real home of *biscotti* or *insalate verde*. So fierce is this local pride that villages have been known to declare war on each other in order to protect their culinary honour! During the sixteenth century, the hilltop town of Sant'Angelo was almost wiped out by neighbouring Fonterenza following a dispute over whether *panzanella* should contain fennel.

Of course, what used to be known as *cucina povera* (or peasant food) is now gaining in popularity, with diners paying big money for the authentic taste of roughly chopped carrots dipped in cheap olive oil. Several Tuscan restaurants have capitalised on this trend by serving very basic food in an impoverished setting, where guests sit on rough crates and eat small servings of simple food from specially cracked designer tableware imported from Turino.

The hardship of Tuscan life fostered an ability to be able to make something out of seemingly nothing, typified by the following recipe I found in a nineteenth-century Florentine cookbook.

Zuppa di Giorno
1 pot boiling water
2 sprigs rosemary (optional)

Bring water to the boil and, if desired,
add rosemary. Serve immediately.

26 May

Today we invited our neighbours Paolo and Mariella over for lunch. Mariella brought a simple salad while Paolo brought his brother Luigi (who also appeared somewhat simple), along with several bottles of homemade *grappa*.

I love the way Italians eat. For them, every meal is to be enjoyed to the full, and they have no time for prim, elbows-in, dainty grazing. Toasting us all around the rough refectory table, Paolo declared, 'This is, how you say, the lives of the party!' which is, of course, not how we say it but his infectious enthusiasm more than made up for any grammatical inadequacies.

To mark our first full week at Villa del Vecchio (and, perhaps, feeling just a touch homesick), I decided to bake a celebratory cake, using one of my grandmother's favourite recipes.

Like most Tuscans, Paulo and Mariella use their land to its fullest. Naturally there is a vegetable garden as well as herbs in pots everywhere you look. Olive trees and other fruit trees cover the open spaces, leaving barely enough room for a few ancient grapevines. Ducks and geese graze noisily while in the shed lives a rather contented cow along with two illegal Senegalese immigrants, who perform odd jobs in return for the Pasquinis keeping quiet.

TORTA DI LAMPONI E CIOCCOLATO DI EUNICE

EUNICE'S CHOCOLATE AND RASPBERRY CAKE

My grandmother was a dedicated, if somewhat eccentric cook. She would often start a dish, then get distracted by a phone call or visiting tradesman, completely forgetting what she was making by the time she returned to it. In these moments, simple casseroles could suddenly be dusted with icing sugar and spooned into a bowl to be served up as a rich – if somewhat unconventional – veal sorbet. Fortunately, this wonderful cake of hers is just about distraction-proof.

200 G DARK CHOCOLATE, CHOPPED

100 G UNSALTED BUTTER, MELTED

5 LARGE EGGS, SEPARATED

$^1/_2$ CUP CASTER SUGAR

$^1/_3$ CUP SELF-RAISING FLOUR, SIFTED

$^1/_2$ CUP HAZELNUTS, GROUND

60 ML FRANGELICO LIQUEUR

RASPBERRY SAUCE

125 G RASPBERRIES

3 TABLESPOONS ICING SUGAR

1. Preheat oven to 190°C.

2. Melt the chocolate and butter over a pot of hot water. Remove from heat and stir in the egg yolks, sugar, flour, hazelnuts and Frangelico, mixing until soft and creamy. Beat the egg whites until firm peaks form.

3. Fold the egg whites lightly into the chocolate mixture and pour into a greased and lined round 20 cm springform cake tin.

4. Bake for 40–45 minutes or until the cake shrinks slightly from the side of the tin.

5. To make the raspberry sauce, place the raspberries and icing sugar in a food processor or blender and purée until smooth. Strain. Add a little water if the mixture is too thick, which it won't be if you've followed my instructions properly.

6. Serve the cake, cut into wedges, with raspberry sauce and a jaunty dollop of cream.

AUDREY'S TIP

When it comes to melting the chocolate, I recommend using a triple boiler – that is, a saucepan inside a saucepan inside a saucepan. Good-quality chocolate is simply too precious to risk burning.

27 May   I am, officially, in heaven! Life here at Villa del Vecchio is simply so relaxed. Each day, Phillip and I wake at dawn to the sound of birdsong: plovers, larks, sparrows, shrikes, and an unusual rasping noise that we thought might be some sort of crow but has subsequently turned out to be Signor Pasquini clearing his throat next door.

There's no doubting it, the pace of life here is much slower than what most of us are used to. The shops all shut at lunchtime and the *siesta* tradition is so seriously maintained that it's illegal to sound a car horn between the hours of 2pm and 4 pm.

The lengthy lunchtime siesta means that Italians can enjoy a hearty meal of pasta or meat, often washed down with a carafe (or three!) of local vino, before wandering back to work. For this reason, it's best to avoid catching a plane or agreeing to undergo delicate surgical procedures in the afternoon.

Similarly, meals are lovingly prepared and made to be lingered over. Unlike back home, where we are often eating on the run, snacking in the car or eating takeaway food in front of the television, Italian children are trained from an early age to remain seated at the table until the head of the family has either finished eating or passed away.

Siesta time in San Cisterno.

'I think one of the saddest aspects of modern life is the demise of the family dinner — instead, young people eat microwaved meals in front of the television, or snack on takeaway food while rushing out the door. Children should be taught from an early age to sit at the dinner table for an hour or more. Obviously, it helps if you give them food, but there's no need to dumb it down with cheese sandwiches or chicken nuggets! If needed, try preparing a few word games or, at the very least, conversation topics to keep the little ones from wandering off. Failing that, a restraining harness can be invaluable...'

28 May It's still raining but the signs of spring are definitely here. Most of the fruit trees are coming into bud and Phillip's sinuses have started to play up, so we know it won't be long now!

As well as cooking for ourselves, Phillip and I have taken the opportunity to sample some local restaurants. Just off the town's main square we discovered a simply exquisite eatery, Silvio's, that was established back in the 1950s by the late Silvio Abrunno. Still very much a family affair, Silvio's widow Grazia greets customers at the door, while his children all work in the kitchen. And despite his death a few years ago, Silvio's presence can still very much be felt. Perhaps it's the stern-looking portrait staring down at diners, or the fact that his body remains in the cool room, while his family saves for a suitably impressive headstone.

I ate a beautiful dish of aubergines and tomato that I simply had to try out for myself at home.

SILVIO ABRUNNO – FOOD HERO

The late Silvio Abrunno was one of the first of what we now know as 'celebrity chefs'. During the 1930s he hosted a cooking programme on the radio and was known as *Cuoco delle Onde*, or 'cook of the airwaves'. From what I can gather, the show simply consisted of Silvio reading out recipes while an audio assistant made noises with cutlery, but it was compulsory listening for Italians. What's more, during the German occupation, his radio programme played a vital role in broadcasting strategic information to allied troops. Silvio only had to mention the word 'anchovies' to trigger a major partisan uprising.

MELANZANE CON POMODORI AL FORNO
BAKED AUBERGINES AND TOMATOES

Interestingly, aubergines aren't native to Italy. They originally came from Asia, along with chillies, capsicums and the tour group we were seated next to at dinner last night. Funny, isn't it, the way people at a large table so quickly forget that they are out and start treating a restaurant like their own private dining room? I wouldn't mind the raised voices so much if they'd at least have the courtesy to speak in Italian or English.

OLIVE OIL

2 LARGE AUBERGINES, CUT INTO HALVES
   AND SCOOPED

1 HEAPED TEASPOON DRIED OREGANO

SEA SALT

FRESHLY GROUND BLACK PEPPER

1 SMALL RED ONION, FINELY CHOPPED

2 CLOVES GARLIC, FINELY SLICED

2–3 TABLESPOONS BEST-QUALITY HERB VINEGAR

5 LARGE RIPE TOMATOES, ROUGHLY CHOPPED

1 SMALL BUNCH FRESH FLAT-LEAF PARSLEY,
   TO GARNISH

1. Pour a few glugs of olive oil into a large pan and heat. Add the aubergine chunks and oregano, season with a little salt and pepper, and cook for around 5 minutes.

2. When the aubergines are well browned, add the onion, garlic and a handful of anchovies. (I know they're not listed in the ingredients section, but I didn't want to dissuade you from at least trying the dish. And, now that you've cooked the aubergines and chopped the tomatoes, there's no real point in going back, is there?)

3. Drizzle the herb vinegar over everything, then add the tomatoes and simmer for around 15 minutes.

4. Serve sprinkled with chopped parsley and another drizzle of olive oil.

AUDREY'S TIP

Some people think this dish can be improved by adding a few tablespoons of lightly toasted slivered almonds. They are wrong.

29 May

Unfortunately, our hot water system shows no sign of being fixed, despite frequent visits by Signor Limbardi. This week he brought his son along to help, if you could call sitting under a tree sending text messages 'helping'. The problem is apparently air in the pipes but we've been assured it will be rectified within a few days, once a small part arrives from Rome.

To complicate matters, we've had some surprise visitors – our old friends Margaret and Jeremy Sanderson. We'd told them to drop by 'anytime', not thinking it would be quite so soon, but they rang from Florence on Thursday saying they were in the area and could they pop in? Despite the somewhat chaotic state of affairs (I'm still unpacking the kitchen utensils and yet to find a whisk!), we couldn't say no and they arrived a short while later.

A disappointing start to spring.

'I love sharing my knowledge and passion for food with others, whether in a formal setting such as one of my Master Classes or simply over a casual supper with friends. Yet can you believe that some of my friends are actually reluctant to invite me around for dinner? They say they are frightened I am going to spend the entire evening criticising every aspect of the meal! I can assure you, this is not my style. And you know what? I find that – as a rule – people want to be told what they're doing wrong. Otherwise, how can anyone expect to learn? Naturally, I'll couch any criticism in very gentle terms and always try to find something positive to focus on, such as the placemats or garden lighting.'

30 May

To celebrate the arrival of our first official house guests, I decided to make veal *ragù*, a dish that relies heavily on the quality of its meat. As a cook, I cannot stress strongly enough the importance of having a good butcher. He can be the difference between disaster and triumph. We have a little Greek man back home, I can never remember his name (let alone pronounce it!), but he looks after my needs.

Fortunately, I've discovered an equally excellent butcher right here in San Cisterno, in the form of Signor Dario Pezzimenti. A self-confessed carnivore, Dario's interest in meat goes back many years to when he was working at a medical research centre harvesting tumours from laboratory mice. His *macelleria* is one of the finest – and most popular – butchers shops in the region.

Back at the villa, Margaret and Jeremy had wasted little time in settling in. In fact, I returned to find Jeremy asleep on the couch. Naturally, I didn't mean to wake him, but his feet were on the coffee table and he stirred just as I was slipping some plastic matting under them.

Dario specialises in offal and, according to Mariella, many San Cisterno housewives will come from miles away just for his tongue.

Our first official house guests, Margaret and Jeremy Sanderson, enjoying some Tuscan sun!

PAPPARDELLE CON VITELLO RAGÙ
PAPPARDELLE WITH VEAL RAGÙ

Veal is Tuscany's most popular meat, closely followed by road kill, and there are many different ways to prepare it. This method involves making a *ragú* (or sauce) and serving it with pasta. *Pappardelle* is very much like *tagliatelle*, but thicker and satisfyingly harder to pronounce.

455 G FINELY GROUND SEMOLINA FLOUR,
    PLUS EXTRA FOR DUSTING
200 ML WATER

RAGÙ SAUCE
OLIVE OIL
1 RED ONION, FINELY CHOPPED
2 CLOVES GARLIC, FINELY CHOPPED
3 BAY LEAVES
SPRIG OF FRESH ROSEMARY
500 G MINCED VEAL
4 × 400 G CANS ITALIAN PLUM TOMATOES
SEA SALT
FRESHLY GROUND BLACK PEPPER
FRESHLY GRATED PARMESAN, TO SERVE

1. Place the flour in a bowl and mix in cold water, a little at a time, to make a stiff dough.

2. Dust a clean work surface with flour and knead the pasta for 10 minutes or so until smooth and velvety. Wrap in cling film and refrigerate until you are ready to use it, which should be now.

3. Pull off an orange-sized piece of pasta dough and use your hands to roll it into a flattened sheet, the thinner the better. Using a sharp knife, cut the sheet into 1 cm wide ribbons. Repeat with the rest of the dough. Lay the *pappardelle* on a tray to allow it to dry out slightly before using.

4. To make the *ragù* sauce, heat some olive oil in a large saucepan. Add the chopped onion and garlic, and cook slowly for about 10 minutes until soft and lightly coloured. Add the bay leaves, rosemary, minced veal and tomatoes. Stir well and bring to the boil. Turn down the heat and simmer gently for 2 hours with the lid on. If the sauce starts to stick at any point, you can add a splash of water and stir, or throw the whole thing out and start again. Season well with salt and freshly ground pepper.

5. Cook the *pappardelle* in boiling salted water for 8–10 minutes until *al dente*.

6. Drain and stir the pasta into the hot *ragù* sauce. Add a good splash of olive oil and season again if necessary (which it won't be if you've followed my instructions carefully). Serve with freshly grated parmesan.

AUDREY'S TIP

If you can't get fresh garlic – those sweet-smelling raggedy bulbs – simply use a clove of ordinary garlic and slightly lower your expectations.

31 May With no sign of our hot water system being fixed, and more rain forecast, we decided to take the Sandersons for a trip to the nearby medieval village of Mangliano.

Driving through the gates of this ancient walled town, we made our way down a cobbled street where Phillip was lucky enough to find a park outside a crumbling stone building. It must have been very old, as there was a Latin inscription on the wall, but none of us were able to make it out (so much for a classical education!).

Not having been there before, we decided to take a tour of Mangliano with an English-speaking guide. At least, that was the claim made by the Turismo official. As it turned out, Francesca seemed to know very little English, simply gesticulating at various monuments and mumbling, 'You look now'. Mind you, her language skills improved remarkably when it came time to explaining the need for a generous tip.

After our tour we settled in for lunch at a small *trattoria* that was recommended in Margaret's guidebook as being 'at the heart of Tuscany's slow food movement'. Unfortunately, it also turned out to be at the heart of its slow service movement, with our main dishes taking over forty minutes to arrive, by which time Phillip and I were almost passing out with hunger (thank God for *grissini!*).

To make matters worse, upon returning to our car we discovered it had been wheel clamped (it turned out that the Latin inscription read 'No Parking'). We had little choice but to pay the somewhat exorbitant fine before making our way slowly back home.

The Sandersons relax after a long day of sightseeing while Phillip and I are in the kitchen preparing dinner and discussing the best way of getting shoe scuff marks off a leather couch.

'I love spring. As the land wakens from its long winter sleep and colourful bulbs seem to flower overnight, life takes on a brighter tone. Small things that might once have upset one, such as slow service at a restaurant or houseguests who leave sodden hand towels on the bathroom floor (as if some maid is going to come in and clean up the mess!), are somehow not quite so aggravating.'

Giugno
june

1 June A waft of aftershave and tobacco smoke this morning told us that Signor Limbardi was coming up the driveway. After several hours (and much cursing), the hot water was still not working, to which Signor Limbardi kept saying, '*No problema.*' Well, I'm sorry, but there is a *problema*! I'm all for rustic charm, but constantly having to heat water in pots on the old wood stove is simply too time consuming.

To make matters worse, Phillip and I have both picked up slight head colds, courtesy (we suspect) of Margaret, who was sneezing frequently throughout her stay with us. She and Jeremy left this afternoon and, while we enjoyed their company, it's nice to have the house back to ourselves.

Phillip has announced plans to build me a wood-fired pizza oven on the back terrace, which should be simply heavenly. We just have to get rid of an old, tumble-down barn to make some room and we should be cooking *al fresco* within weeks. Very exciting.

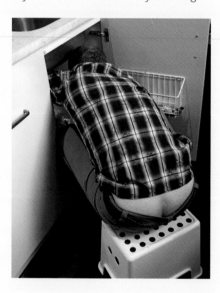

Signor Limbardi – an all too familiar sight.

RAVIOLI DI SPINACI
SPINACH RAVIOLI

Ravioli would have to be one of my favourite forms of pasta, whether stuffed with meat, vegetables, cheese or seafood. And while it's possible to find perfectly adequate store-bought varieties, nothing beats the taste and sense of quiet superiority that comes with making your own.

500 G UNBLEACHED PLAIN WHEAT FLOUR

4 LARGE EGGS (ORGANIC IF POSSIBLE)

1 TEASPOON SALT

RICOTTA FILLING

1 KG SPINACH LEAVES, UNWASHED*

2 CUPS FRESH RICOTTA

2 EGGS

150 G PARMESAN, FRESHLY GRATED

DASH OF GRATED NUTMEG

SALT

FRESHLY GROUND BLACK PEPPER

* Tuscans greatly value the added 'crunch' that comes from soil residue.

1. Heap the flour into a mound on a large marble pastry slab (available at most funeral supply shops) and make a well in the centre. Break the eggs into it, adding a generous dash of salt, and using your hand as a 'paddle' (fingers together) combine the ingredients. Continue kneading until the pasta is smooth or elastic (but not both), then divide into two balls. Cover in cling film (preferably organic) and set aside for 30 minutes, which should give you just enough time to clean up the bits of dried pasta caking every nearby surface.

2. To make the filling, place the spinach in a large saucepan of boiling water and cook for 8–10 minutes, then drain and chop finely. In a large mixing bowl combine the spinach with the ricotta, eggs, parmesan, nutmeg, salt and pepper.

3. On a floured work surface, roll out each piece of pasta to paper thin, then cut into 8 cm squares. Place 2 teaspoons of filling in the centre of each square and gather the edges together, pinching firmly.

4. Place the ravioli in a pot of boiling water and cook until they rise to the surface or collapse and sink to the bottom.

AUDREY'S TIP

To seal the individual parcels you can brush the edges lightly with egg, but the traditional method is spit. Simply moisten one finger in your mouth and brush the edges of the pasta. Or, if you want to be totally authentic, it is now possible to purchase small bottles of certified Tuscan Saliva at many speciality stores.

2 June   Unfortunately, the rain has lingered on, making it difficult for us to get outside. The lack of hot water is beginning to become a real issue and I've left several quite terse messages on S. Limbardi's phone demanding that he do something about it.

With our kitchen cupboards just about bare, we braved the weather to make a dash into town for urgent supplies. However, just as we arrived, the midday church bells chimed and, on cue, every shopkeeper closed his doors and pulled down the shutters, indicating *siesta* time had begun.

Now, I'm all for maintaining ancient traditions, but I honestly feel there needs to be some degree of flexibility here, especially in the retail sector. Despite our tapping on the window of Signor Cortona's store, he deliberately chose to ignore us and we were forced to return home empty-handed. Of course, this is where the true home cook comes into her own! With no milk and limited groceries, I was still able to come up with a satisfying evening meal.

I could tell there was someone in the back of the shop but getting them to open up was another thing.

PAPPA AL POMODORO
TOMATO AND BREAD SOUP

If there's one thing I can't emphasise enough in this book, it's the importance of freshness. In Italy, the women shop daily, even if it is just for shoes, but most will also make at least one stop to buy fresh produce. And each day's menu is planned around what looks, feels and smells to be in peak condition. If nothing appears up to standard, they would rather starve. This recipe calls for only the very freshest basil.

600 G FIRM RIPE TOMATOES

10 TABLESPOONS EXTRA-VIRGIN OLIVE OIL, PLUS EXTRA FOR SERVING

3 CLOVES GARLIC, PEELED AND BRUISED

500 ML WATER OR STOCK

250 G STALE BREAD,* CUT INTO THICK SLICES

SALT

FRESHLY GROUND BLACK PEPPER

8–10 FRESH BASIL LEAVES, PLUS EXTRA TO GARNISH

In England we feed stale bread to the pigeons. Here in Tuscany, this bread (and, quite often, the pigeons too) will be used for cooking.

1. Place the tomatoes in a heatproof bowl. Add sufficient boiling water to cover and leave for 1 minute. Drain, rinse quickly in cold water, then skin the tomatoes. Cut them in half, remove the seeds and any tough parts, and chop into small pieces.

2. Heat a glug of olive oil in a large pot and add the garlic, frying until softened. Add the tomatoes, along with 2 cups of water or stock, and bring to the boil. Simmer for 15 minutes.

3. Tear the bread into thumb-sized pieces and add to the pot. Mix well and season before tearing in the basil leaves, gently cooking for another 10 minutes.

4. Add another glug of olive oil and stir – you should have a thick, velvety consistency, much like porridge. Remove from the heat and add another 6–7 tablespoons of extra-virgin olive oil.

5. Serve in individual bowls with a little extra basil torn over the top.

AUDREY'S TIP

Most people use sea salt but I prefer rock salt as it has a slightly less salty taste.

3 June

The pool is starting to turn an unfortunate shade of green. Phillip thinks there might be mosquitoes breeding in it. Signor Pasquini has kindly offered to come over and take a look while his wife has promised to offer up prayers.

In news from home, this year's Queen's Birthday Honours have been announced and it seems that Rick Stein has received another award, this time for 'service to food'. Naturally, I'm delighted for him; it's wonderful when anyone in our industry is given due recognition for their efforts. However, I can't help feeling there could be more worthy recipients. When you look at what Phillip and I have done for the UK culinary scene over two decades, it seems baffling that our efforts have once again been overlooked in favour of an overpriced fish 'n' chip shop in Padstow. Still, that's why we came here to Tuscany, to get away from the stress and and annoyances of daily life. Time for a relaxing walk and a calming Campari to weave their magic while we forget all about such petty grievances.

What a wreck!

OLIVE OIL – TUSCANY'S LIQUID GOLD

While there is evidence of Roman civilisation just about everywhere you look in Tuscany, it was in fact the ancient Greeks who first settled this region. Here, in ancient palaces, wealthy nobles would gather for regular feasts – not to mention orgies! The Greeks were followed by the Romans, who took this tradition of orgies to a new level – by including women. But it was the Greeks who planted Tuscany's first olive groves, many of which still survive to this day.

Extra-virgin olive oil is highly prized, and is used to dress salads, to preserve vegetables and fish, and to enliven a wide range of *antipasti* dishes. In some remote villages, olive oil is believed to be capable of raising the dead or, at the very least, making them more presentable for viewing.

'Extra virgin' refers to the oil extracted from the first, cold pressing of the olives. In fact, these olives are not actually pressed at all; the oil is simply coaxed out with gentle music and mood lighting. Any remaining oil, being of an inferior quality, is extracted chemically and used for deep frying, or as personal lubricant.

4 June   Then there's our selfless charity work and social justice campaigns. For the past five years I've sat on the board of *Breakout!*, an international collective lobbying for a ban on waxed lemons. Where's the recognition for that?

Up early for a trip to the *mercato centrale* (or central market). I simply *love* shopping here. It's a real experience watching the locals engaged in animated repartee with their favourite vendors. You need not understand *Italiano* – facial expressions, body language and wild gesticulations say it all. And everything is so fresh! Honestly, I couldn't even *look* at a supermarket tomato. Speaking with each stallholder, sampling their produce, learning about where it came from – this is what shopping is all about.

This morning I got chatting to a cheese-maker at the market, who told me his future was doubtful as the big factories, producers of industrial cheese, were competing with the small artisans. On top of that, taxes and production costs were constantly rising, making it difficult for people like him to survive. It was a fascinating insight into agrarian life, but after about twenty minutes this gloomy discussion began to get a little tiresome and I sidled off in search of broad beans (where I was informed that the legume industry was also under threat).

Audrey's
dinner party etiquette

Whether dining *al fresco* in our Tuscan garden or eating *chez vous* in a more humdrum domestic setting of your own, there is nothing quite like the simple pleasure of entertaining friends at home. But when it comes to being part of such social gatherings, either as a host or a guest, there are rules to ensure that the event runs smoothly.

I know it's an old-fashioned word, but understanding basic dinner party etiquette can make all the difference. Throughout this book, I have offered some of the simple guidelines I've gathered over the years that are, in my opinion, worth bearing in mind.

Planning

Even the most casual of dinner parties requires months of planning, preparation and stress. Remember, a perfectly organised event can be ruined by a carelessly folded napkin. The key is to prepare ahead so that you are not tied to the kitchen, but free to mingle with your guests and soak in their accolades.

Lists

When planning a dinner party, I find it useful to keep lists. Start with your guests. For certain events there will be some people that one simply must invite: close family, business associates, anyone connected with the media. Note down any dietary preferences or restrictions, and a rough estimate of how much each of them will typically consume (there's no greater nightmare for a host than the thought that you might have under-catered!). Be especially wary of anyone who tells you that they are 'on a diet' – these people tend to possess the most ravenous appetites of all.

Hired help

When numbers exceed a dozen, it is often necessary (and wise!) to hire waiting staff. But in doing so there needs to be very clear boundaries. While these people are in your home, they must be reminded that they are not guests but casual employees. Joining in conversations, expressing opinions or lingering in a room to enjoy the entertainment on offer is not part of their job description, and any attempts to do so should be viewed as a serious overstepping of the mark. Never pay in advance, and remind them that you reserve the right to dock pay for surliness, clumsiness or inappropriate piercings.

5 June

Well, summer is here at last, bringing with it an abundance of fresh produce in the markets. It's a wondrous time, as the days begin to lengthen and the land wakes from its long winter slumber. Which makes it particularly frustrating that so many shops still remain closed. Apparently they are yet to re-open after the winter break but we've been assured they will do so any day now.

For dinner tonight I decided to cook rabbit, ordering the meat from a local game supplier. To our horror the rabbits arrived soon after – alive! Fortunately, Mariella was able to drop by from next door and 'dispatch' them for us, meaning all I had to do was put the oven on and clean up the blood.

Rabbit is a great favourite in Tuscany, and most households keep a few in the back garden. They make ideal pets as well as ingredients, meaning that Italian children are encouraged to play with their food.

'Many young people have lost a sense of understanding of where their food comes from. If you ask me, there's nothing quite like the experience of rearing, feeding, caring for and then butchering your own pets...'

CONIGLIO MARINATO ALLA GRIGLIA
GRILLED AND MARINATED RABBIT

This simple yet flavoursome dish is seasoned with herbs and lemon juice. We also added a few tablespoons of Signor Pasquini's homemade *grappa*. If you can't find any *grappa*, half a cup of cough medicine should achieve similar results.

1 × 1.2 KG RABBIT, PREFERABLY WILD,* JOINTED

HANDFUL FRESH THYME AND ROSEMARY LEAVES

4 CLOVES GARLIC, PEELED

OLIVE OIL

ZEST AND JUICE OF 1 LEMON

3 TABLESPOONS GRAPPA (OPTIONAL)

SALT

FRESHLY GROUND BLACK PEPPER

3 THICK SLICES PANCETTA

* While farmed rabbits are tender and juicy, there's no doubting that the wild variety has a more intense flavour. Tuscans love the authentic taste of wild game and many will view with suspicion any animal that looks as if it has died non-violently.

1. Place the rabbit pieces in a bowl.

2. Using a pestle and mortar, pulverise the thyme and rosemary leaves to a pulp. Add the garlic cloves and continue to pulverise before stirring in the olive oil, lemon zest, juice and *grappa* (if using).

3. Pour the marinade over the rabbit and put to one side while you light your barbecue.

4. Season the pieces of meat with salt and pepper. Wrap the belly pieces in pancetta, securing with skewers.

5. Place the larger pieces of rabbit (legs and shoulder) on the barbecue first, followed by the belly, saddle and ribs. Make sure to keep turning the meat and basting with marinade as needed until cooked.

AUDREY'S TIP

I prefer farmed, free-range rabbit but here in Tuscany wild rabbit is commonly eaten. Wild rabbit has a stronger taste and can be a little tough. It's also often full of shot gun pellets and should be avoided by anyone who is lead intolerant.

6 June

Tragic news from home: one of Phillip's closest old schoolfriends has suffered a severe asthma attack and died. On the plus side – white asparagus has appeared at the market!

After several weeks living here in the heart of Tuscany, I have come up with some simple tips for the visitor.

1. Go with the flow.
2. Embrace simplicity and change.
3. Don't hire G. Limbardi & Sons to do any of your plumbing work.

Honestly, a more inept or malodorous tradesman would be hard to find. After yet another 'flushing out' of our hot water system this morning, Signor Limbardi emerged from underneath the house to announce that most of the copper piping was missing, presumably 'stolen by gypsies'. Information that might have been useful three weeks ago! Naturally, he's promised to have the problem fixed by Friday (where have I heard that before?) but we now face the prospect of another week without hot water.

7 June

Phillip's sister Helena arrived somewhat unexpectedly today. Naturally, we're both delighted to see her but things are still rather chaotic around here. I've got people in measuring the kitchen for a new oven (while I love the old wood stove to bits, it's proving a little too temperamental for regular use) and Phillip thinks the pool might be giving off some sort of hazardous gas. Still, it will be good having an extra pair of hands to help around the property. Helena is a children's book illustrator, or – at least – hopes to be once she can convince someone of her talents, and Phillip is very fond of her.

Speaking of my darling husband, the poor lamb has had a setback building his wood-fired pizza oven as we've been refused permission to demolish the old barn. Apparently, it's extremely old and under some sort of Government 'cultural heritage' listing (it's a pile of bricks!). Despite our offer to put up a plaque, the authorities won't allow us to knock it down. Hopefully we can find another suitable site for the oven.

'To my mind there can be no greater crime than overcooking fish. Like cruelty to animals and genocide, it's simply unforgiveable...'

8 June

On one of our first mornings at Villa del Vecchio, our neighbour Mariella showed up with a huge basket laden with sun-dried tomatoes, herbs, homemade sauces and a bottle of extra-virgin olive oil. For newly arrived visitors like us, it was an absolute godsend and as I write this, I'm pleased to say, that basket of goodies is still sitting in our kitchen. Unfortunately, so too is Mariella, whose arrival each morning has become a regular feature of life here. It's not that we don't enjoy her company, but there's simply so much work to be done around the place.

We've managed to clear most of the rubbish out of the downstairs rooms and Phillip has prepared the walls for painting. Unfortunately, Helena has been unable to help due to 'back spasms', which apparently make any sort of movement extremely painful so she's largely been confined to resting, reading and dessert.

Helena, hard at work.

POLLO ARROSTO CON AGLIO E PASTA D'ERBE
ROAST CHICKEN WITH GARLIC AND HERB PASTE

This recipe was first shown to me by my dear friend Toni Lyons at the Beaumont Brasserie, and I've included it here as a tribute to her friendship and tenacity. Toni is living proof that with hard work and determination (not to mention wealthy parents), *anyone* can run a successful restaurant. The 'Beau' was for years a staple of London's food scene, catering to those who wanted a good, reliable, unchallenging dining experience. I've respectfully made a few changes to Toni's version (I wouldn't go so far as to call them 'improvements'!) that should, I hope, greatly improve the finished product.

AUDREY'S TIP

Wrap cloves of garlic, sprigs of rosemary, fillips of tarragon and tranchettes of onion in a muslin cloth. If you don't happen to have any muslin on hand then any clean cloth will do. My mother often used her old pantyhose, which gave the dish a delightfully piquant acidity.

I LARGE HEAD OF GARLIC

I × I.4 KG CHICKEN

I LEMON, PEELED AND CUT IN HALF

I ORANGE, PEELED AND CUT IN HALF

4 CARROTS, HALVED LENGTHWAYS

SALT

FRESHLY GROUND BLACK PEPPER

6 TABLESPOONS EXTRA-VIRGIN OLIVE OIL

50 G BUTTER, SOFTENED, AT ROOM TEMPERATURE

80 ML WHITE WINE

80 ML CHICKEN STOCK

8 SAGE LEAVES, FINELY CHOPPED

2 SPRIGS ROSEMARY, NEEDLES ONLY, FINELY CHOPPED

3 SPRIGS THYME, LEAVES ONLY, FINELY CHOPPED

I TABLESPOON VERY FINELY CHOPPED PARSLEY

1. Preheat oven to 200°C.

2. Place the unpeeled garlic cloves in a hot oven for 15 minutes until soft. Remove the skins and mix the puréed garlic to form a paste.

3. Take the chicken and carefully ease the skin away from the breasts, taking care not to tear the skin. With your fingers, spread the garlic paste evenly over the breast underneath the skin. Fill the cavity of the chicken with the lemon and orange halves.

4. Line the bottom of your roasting tray with carrots.

5. Rub the chicken well all over with butter as if applying sunscreen.

6. Place the chicken on the bed of carrots, season with salt and pepper and then lightly drizzle with olive oil. Pour in the wine and stock, along with the herbs.

5. Cover with foil and roast.

'I am passionate about food and love sharing my knowledge with other people. For me, there is no greater pleasure than helping someone who is taking their first steps as a cook realise just how little they know.'

9 June After weeks of electronic-free bliss, we finally had the internet connected today and, almost at once, I came to regret it, with an email from my producer back in London saying that ITV have apparently decided to 'pass' on the series we piloted back in March. Not that I care all that much for the idea of being on television; I think the world has more than enough would-be celebrity chefs peddling their various brands of kitchen philosophy. But every now and then a concept comes along that is both intelligent and original. That's why I was so excited about taking part in *Blind, Dumb and Chef*, combining as it did my love of authentic regional cuisine with a studio-based game show format. However, it seems that certain commissioning editors found it 'offensive' to the hearing impaired (this despite the fact that we were all only pretending that the orders were inaudible and had to be mimed). I give up. Still, who'd want to be in some cramped television studio when they could be here, enjoying a Tuscan summer?

The skies are showing definite signs of clearing. Summer can't be far!

PURÈ DI PATATE
AUDREY'S MASHED POTATO

All right, I know it's not strictly a Tuscan dish, but there are times when we all crave a bit of traditional comfort food. And what could be more nourishing on an unseasonally cool June night than a steaming bowl of mashed spud? This is best made in a big pan, with a large, heavy bottom. Speaking of which, Helena is still here and shows no sign of moving on, despite her initial claim that it was 'just for a couple of days'.

75 G WARM FULL-FAT MILK

4 TABLESPOONS CREAM

50 G BUTTER

2 EGGS

1/2 CUP FINELY GRATED PARMESAN

POTATOES (OPTIONAL)

1. Gently heat the milk, cream and butter in a large saucepan.

2. Add the eggs and parmesan and stir to combine.

3. If using potatoes, peel and boil them before mashing and adding to the milk and butter mixture. Serve immediately.

10 June Well, the rain has finally stopped but it's still a little too cool to eat outside. Phillip has managed to rig up a couple of gas burners that have allowed us to enjoy the occasional lunch *al fresco*, provided no one lingers too long and we don't mind wearing gloves, but on the whole dining has been confined to indoors.

Of course, it won't be long before the weather lifts; summer is definitely on its way and Phillip has been busy in the back garden building our wood-fired pizza oven. All the stone is now in place and Signor Pasquini has been over helping to mix the cement, cheekily informing us that it must be 'very thick – just like you English!' He has a delightful sense of humour. Sadly, no such progress on the hot water front, with Signor Limbardi informing us that the replacement copper piping will not be here until Thursday.

Helena returned from town this morning, armed with a basket of groceries, and proceeded to cook what she called 'Tuscan soup'. I had to laugh as the resulting dish was nothing like a Tuscan soup, more a watery stew. Naturally, I didn't say (or eat) anything, but I couldn't resist producing my own slightly more authentic version for supper tonight, just to help her gain a clear understanding of the actual difference.

Phillip enjoying some outdoor dining.

ZUPPA SEMPLICE
SIMPLE SOUP

This flavoursome soup can be made with bacon but I much prefer genuine *pancetta*, even if it is a little harder to find. Ask your local butcher. If he doesn't have it, ask him to order some in and say you'll be back. Naturally, you shouldn't ever shop there again. It will teach him a lesson and, hopefully, spare his next customer the disappointment of an inadequate smallgoods range.

125 ML OLIVE OIL

1 SMALL BUNCH SILVERBEET

3 STICKS CELERY

4 CARROTS, CUT INTO 5 MM CHUNKS

2 SMALL RED ONIONS, COARSELY CHOPPED

1 CLOVES GARLIC, CHOPPED

1/2 CUP FINELY CHOPPED PARSLEY

8 SLICES PANCETTA, CUT INTO STRIPS

250 G PARMESAN RIND, CUT INTO LARGE
   CHUNKS

1.5 LITRES HOMEMADE STOCK

SALT

FRESHLY GROUND BLACK PEPPER

2 × 400 G CANS ITALIAN TOMATOES,
   JUICES RETAINED

1. Heat the olive oil in a large ovenproof pot. Add the silverbeet, celery, carrots, onions, tomatoes, garlic and parsley and cook over medium heat for 8–10 minutes, stirring occasionally.

2. Add the pancetta and parmesan rind, then cover with stock. Season to taste. Bring to a boil and cook for a further 20 minutes.

AUDREY'S TIP

There's no doubting you can tell the worth of a chef by their stock. Good chefs have at least three large pots of it on the go, made fresh every morning from fish, meat, vegetables and perhaps chicken. I often have a fourth which is lemon scented and used for washing up. Now I know you can purchase all sorts of pre-made varieties of stock but I urge you – before reaching for some over-salted, artificially coloured cube of chemicals: think. How will I feel about yourself in the morning? Homemade stock not only enriches a soup or sauce, it enriches life. It *is* life, in all its bubbling, roiling, broiling, nurturing, warmed goodness. I love stock.

11 June
With the gradually improving weather, Phillip and I took the opportunity today to explore a little further afield. We visited a charming little cheese factory on the outskirts of Montefollonico, where the local speciality pecorino is lovingly handmade by Maurizio Pieroni.

I love buying produce from a true artisan, and you can tell the genuine version. There's a certain passion in the way they speak, often coupled with a somewhat cavalier approach to personal hygiene that leaves one in no doubt about their commitment to hand-produced food.

Signor Pieroni has been a cheese-maker for over thirty years. In his halting English he explained that, for him, making cheese was like making love, as 'both involved sheep'. We left soon after, but not before buying some delightfully aged pecorino that had been stored in walnut leaves, giving it a unique yet subtle flavour. I couldn't wait to get home and try it.

12 June
On the way back from the market this morning, we popped in for lunch at La Gibrala, a small *trattoria* that our neighbours Paolo and Mariella had recommended highly. According to them, the owner and chef Aldo had spent the past five years working at some of the finest hotels in Paris. (What they didn't mention was that he'd been working there as a cleaner.) That aside, the meal was excellent: grilled sausages with a simple side salad of beetroot and parsnip, followed by some rather decadent nougat slice. We were offered seconds but I had to decline; if I'm not careful with all this wonderful food, it could see me losing what's left of my girlish figure.

La Gibrala

SPAGHETTI AL PESTO
SPAGHETTI PESTO

Pesto. Is there any other ingredient that so perfectly captures the essence of summer? To open and smell a jar of properly made pesto is to be immediately transported to a still, cloudless morning, waking on crisp linen sheets to the sound of ducks foraging in the wood heap for worms while somewhere off in the distance a young shirtless farmhand cuts hay with muscular strokes of his broad, suntanned arms. I love pesto.

I CLOVE GARLIC, CHOPPED

3 HANDFULS CHOPPED FRESH BASIL LEAVES

SEA SALT

HANDFUL PINE NUTS, VERY LIGHTLY TOASTED

HANDFUL FRESHLY GRATED PECORINO,
   PLUS EXTRA TO SERVE

EXTRA-VIRGIN OLIVE OIL

SMALL SQUEEZE OF LEMON JUICE (OPTIONAL)

400 G FRESH SPAGHETTI

FRESHLY GROUND BLACK PEPPER

1. Pound the garlic and basil leaves with a pinch of salt in a mortar and pestle. Add the pine nuts and pound some more. (Some people toast the pine nuts until they're coloured, as this gives them a more nutty taste, but I prefer to just lightly toast them as it brings out more of a buttery creaminess than a nutty nuttiness.)

2. Spoon the mixture into another bowl and add half the cheese, along with a little olive oil. You only need enough oil to bind everything, so don't overdo things.

3. Add the remaining cheese and a little more oil, enough to keep the pesto moist. You might like to add a squeeze of lemon juice at this stage but I don't so neither should you.

4. Bring a pot of lightly salted water to the boil. Add the spaghetti and cook until *al dente*. Drain the pasta and stir through the pesto.

5. Serve with grated pecorino and freshly ground black pepper.

AUDREY'S TIP

Though simple, this makes an ideal light lunch, hearty enough that little else need be served except perhaps a bowl of fresh apricots and some ginger tea. So I was surprised to discover Helena munching hazelnut pralines out on our patio a short while later. Hopefully, your guests will exhibit a little more self-control.

'Remember: anyone can follow a recipe. But unless you're prepared to put your whole self into the dish — heart, soul, hands and, if de-boning a duck, elbows — then you'll never produce something great.'

13 June   Outside at last! This morning the rain finally eased off and by the afternoon we actually had sunshine and clear blue skies! After weeks of eating inside it was time to drag out the table and enjoy a meal *al fresco*. A pumpkin risotto and grilled meats were the simplest of options, washed down with some delightfully sweet *prosecco*. For dessert I served an elegant fruit and cheese platter, featuring some of the pecorino we brought home from Montefollonico.

    Joining us on this special night were Helena, our neighbours Paolo and Mariella, and several ex-pat friends living nearby. Seated outside in the courtyard with a glass of dessert wine, warm breezes wafting up from the olive grove and a silvery moon glowing above, who could ask for anything? Helena, of course, who wanted a more comfortable chair.

Dining al fresco *with friends and neighbours at Villa del Vecchio. As usual, I am being complimented on my food.*

RISOTTO ALLA ZUCCA
PUMPKIN RISOTTO

I can't believe the number of people who are convinced that this quintessential rice dish is impossibly finicky and time consuming. Yes, it must be prepared carefully (I like to individually coat each grain of rice with butter using a small pastry brush), but what decent food is not worth a little effort? And, generally speaking, I find that guests will appreciate the fact that you've gone to a lot of trouble on their behalf.

1. Heat the chicken stock in a saucepan.

2. While the stock is heating, fry the onion, garlic, pumpkin and pancetta in a small amount of olive oil until softened. Add the arborio rice and stir well. At this point, the key is not to leave the pot. Keep stirring NO MATTER WHAT HAPPENS. I've heard of so many uncommitted cooks leaving their stove for the most frivolous of reasons. The fact that a young child *sounds* like they're having a mild asthma attack is simply not a good enough excuse in my book. And no amount of hospital care can save overcooked rice.

3. Gradually add 180 ml hot chicken stock and stir until absorbed. Keep adding the stock, a little at a time, until it is all absorbed. Under no circumstances should this process be rushed or you will end up with a soggy mess.

4. Once the risotto is ready (this will often be indicated when the rice is no longer chalky, and most of your guests have gone home), take it off the heat and stir in the grated parmesan.

5. Lightly steam the broccoli florets, do not overcook.

6. Serve the risotto immediately, garnished with steamed broccoli florets and a sprig of parsley. Or, if you're feeling wistful, a sprinkle of thyme leaves.

1.5 LITRES CHICKEN STOCK

1 ONION, CHOPPED

2 CLOVES GARLIC, CRUSHED

2 CUPS CUBED PUMPKIN

2 FLORETS BROCCOLI, CHOPPPED

2 SLICES PANCETTA, CHOPPED

OLIVE OIL

2 CUPS ARBORIO RICE

4 TABLESPOONS FRESHLY GRATED PARMESAN

PARSLEY OR THYME, TO GARNISH

AUDREY'S TIP

If you're making this dish for vegetarians, either omit the fried pancetta or tell them it's onion.

14 June

Well, summer is truly here at last! After weeks of low cloud and misty rain the skies have finally cleared. Our garden is bursting with growth and I've even been out digging in the vegetable patch. We've also managed to fix the swimming pool. Our dear neighbour Signor Pasquini came over and dosed it with some of his *grappa*, which seems to have killed off most of the bacteria.

Even better, Phillip's wood-fired oven is now finished, although we're having a few 'teething problems'. The main issue seems to be the chimney: it's not drawing properly, which is resulting in excessive smoking. Which reminds me, Signor Limbardi showed up again this afternoon with some replacement piping for our hot water unit. I'd just about given up all hope of it ever being fixed but – touch wood – he seems to be making progress at last.

In terms of guests, Helena has finally left but no sooner had I finished airing out her room than we received news that our dear friends Gerald and Heather Weatherby are on their way over for a short stay. They won't be arriving for a few days but we needed to stock up on provisions. Luckily it was market day and we spent several glorious hours wandering through the various stalls.

When shopping at the market one can learn a lot simply by grabbing what others are buying, even if it means returning home with an unidentified vegetable or mysterious bunch of herbs. Of course, a somewhat more circumspect approach is called for when shopping at the pharmacy.

AUDREY THE GARDENER

Everyone in Tuscany grows their own produce, be it veggies or herbs, and this sense of self-sufficiency is something we could all learn from back home. There's no doubt that in the UK our children have become disconnected from food. To them, a tomato is simply something you buy at a supermarket, rather than a living object grown by human hands. That is, of course, one of the reasons why I set up my School Garden and Kitchen Programme®. The aim was to educate and empower young students with the knowledge that they could grow their own food. And, I'm pleased to say, it was an enormous success, despite one or two minor setbacks. It's funny, isn't it, how the media focus on negatives? Rather than celebrate the *dozens* of schools producing crisp lettuce and juicy carrots for their cafeterias, they had to focus on one small marijuana plot found at a Midlands Polytechnic. Clearly an isolated incident. (And, as I said at the time, at least they were learning about herbs.)

The other claim (equally false) was that we 'abandoned' the garden scheme as soon as the accompanying television series was completed. I still keep in regular contact with many of the schools involved and fully intend to visit them all again when I get the opportunity. But I can hardly be expected to drop by and help with the weeding (as certain school principals have actually suggested). Honestly, there's no pleasing some people.

15 June

The weather continues to be excellent (sorry for all of you stuck at home under grey skies!) and today we drove to a nearby village called Lunogania, where we had lunch at a simply delightful restaurant overlooking the town square.

I enjoyed a heavenly sage risotto while Phillip ordered pan-fried veal served on a bed of flaccid greens. During our meal the owner's son Giacomo appeared with his guitar and played some traditional folk music, a wonderful accompaniment while we enjoyed our main course. By dessert it was starting to get a little monotonous, especially as Giacomo only seemed to know three tunes. (I'm no musician, but does calling something a 'variation' really make it a new song?) Still, we didn't want to say anything rude.

On a disappointing note, we returned home to discover we'd been burgled. Thieves had forced their way in through an open window at the back of our villa and practically stripped the place, stealing money, jewellery, a camera and computer equipment. The blighters even took my favourite Le Creuset tagine, which was a gift from a dear friend.

About the only thing of value they left was a painting of Phillip's that we had hanging above the fireplace (they'll be kicking themselves!). Thankfully, the police say they're pretty sure who was responsible (itinerant Romanian workers) and it's just a question of time before the culprits are apprehended.

Each morning on my way into town we pass this somewhat impressive statue of St Stefano, a greatly revered fourteenth century martyr. For refusing to renounce God his eyes were plucked out, his legs broken and he was then roasted alive over hot coals for a month. It was to be six weeks, but he was apparently given time off for good behaviour.

'I honestly believe that 90 per cent of the world's conflicts could be averted if world leaders simply sat down to share a fragrant tomato and basil salad or, at the very least, started their own compost heap…'

16 June

After a week of glorious sunshine I woke to find the garden enveloped in what appeared to be thick fog. Fearing a return of our wintery weather, I was relieved when it turned out to be Phillip's wood-fired oven. The darling had woken early to get it started so I could bake some bread. Unfortunately, we're still having problems with the chimney; it's not drawing properly and fumes are tainting the food. This is not such a problem with meat or chicken dishes, but heavily smoked meringue is a little less easy to disguise, even with vanilla essence.

Of course, a bit of smoke didn't stop us making the bread. It's amazing how many people think that baking bread is somehow impossibly complex or beyond them. Because of this, perhaps, it seems that home-baked bread has gone the way of darning socks and handwritten thank you notes (did you know we are yet to hear one word from Phillip's sister?). Fortunately, here in Tuscany bread-baking is a tradition that is actively maintained and I, for one, couldn't be happier. I love making bread; it's such an active, tactile, enervating, therapeutic, nurturing process that I defy anyone to not enjoy it. And it's so good for you!

I read recently that some prisons in the United States have been successfully experimenting with bread-baking as a means of rehabilitation. I can't remember the exact figures, but at one institution there was something like a 97 per cent drop in violent crime among those who took part in the programme (the other 3 per cent were executed, resulting in near-perfect results!).

PAOLO'S PANE TOSCANO
PAOLO'S TUSCAN BREAD

Signor Pasquini has been baking bread his entire life and kindly agreed to share this simple recipe. You'll notice there's no salt – Tuscan bread is traditionally baked without salt – but feel free to add a tablespoon if you don't mind trampling on centuries of culinary tradition.

1 KG STRONG BREAD FLOUR, PLUS EXTRA
    FOR DUSTING
625 ML TEPID WATER
30 G FRESH YEAST OR 3 × 7 G SACHETS
    DRIED YEAST
2 TABLESPOONS SUGAR
1 LEVEL TABLESPOON FINE SEA SALT

1. Pile the flour onto a clean surface and make a large well in the centre. Pour half the water into the well, then add the yeast, sugar and salt and stir with a fork. Gradually bring in the flour from the inside of the well. Do this slowly but confidently (remember, yeast is a living organism and can sense when you're tentative).

2. Continue to bring the flour into the centre until you have a porridge-like consistency, then add the remaining water. Continue to mix until it's stodgy again, then bring in the rest of the flour.

3. Now it's time for the kneading! Using a bit of elbow grease, simply push, fold, slap and roll the dough around, over and over, for 4 or 5 minutes until you have a silky and elastic dough. The dough is ready when it forms a soft but firm, flexible ball and springs back when you touch it. 'Like a young girl's breast,' jokes Paolo with a mischievous grin.

4. Flour the top of your dough. Put it in a bowl, cover with cling film, and allow it to prove for about half an hour in a warm, moist, draught-free place. Once the dough has doubled in size it needs to be punched down. 'Just like a disobedient wife!' adds Signor Pasquini with his dry Tuscan humour.

5. You can now shape it as required then leave it to prove for a second time for 30 minutes to an hour, until it has doubled in size once more. During this period I generally take the phone off the hook and keep conversation to a minimum, as any sudden noise or activity could interfere with the proving process.

6. Preheat oven 220°C.

7. Very gently place your bread dough on a flour-dusted baking tray and put in the preheated oven. (Don't even think about slamming the door!) Bake until crisp and slightly browned on top. You can generally tell if it's cooked by tapping its bottom. (I don't feel it's necessary to repeat Signor Pasquini's comment at this point.) If it sounds hollow, it's done.

8. Once the bread is cooked, place it on a rack and allow it to cool for at least 30 minutes.

17 June

The thing I love about the food here is it's so totally seasonal. Most Italians cannot even imagine eating something that has not been grown locally and served in season. At Tuscan restaurants, the menu constantly changes in accordance with what's available. Today we ate at a local *trattoria* and by the time we'd ordered, white cabbage had gone out of season and we were presented with a side serve of *cavalo nero* instead.

Of course, this is a far cry from back home where we expect to be able to buy just about anything, anytime. Sure, it might be convenient but, if you ask me, I think this sense of constant supply comes at a cost. People miss out on the tingling anticipation that comes with the arrival of walnut season or the exquisite excitement of popping that first sweet peach into your mouth. I feel sorry for the youngsters of today who will never know the wistful, bittersweet yearning that comes with realising it's going to be six months until they taste another apricot.

Not far from our house is this beautifully restored villa, now used as an overseas writers retreat. Phillip and I were invited over for afternoon tea one day and we enjoyed meeting the various authors who have come to Tuscany for some 'creative stimulus'. From what I can tell, most of them seemed to be working on novels set in Mumbai. On the day we visited, one writer in residence was very excited because, after weeks of creative effort, he'd finally completed his application for a literary grant.

HOLY DROP

This stunning monastery was built during the fourteenth century, and is home to the Colombite monks. Founded in Siena, the Colombites were known as a 'discalced' order, in that they went without shoes, a symbol of their strict poverty. Around 1480 a breakaway group attempted to also go without pants, but they were quickly relegated to kitchen duties.

These days the Colombites are better known for their famous liqueur Aqua Dieu, or 'Water of God'. First blended during the sixteenth century, the distinctive drink was originally marketed as the 'elixir of life', a claim that had to be withdrawn after several hundred people died from drinking the first batch. Brewing standards were subsequently improved and Aqua Dieu has gone on to become the region's signature drink. Essentially a herbal liqueur, Aqua Dieu contains twenty-seven different ingredients. For centuries, its recipe was a closely guarded secret, until a printing error led to the ingredients being listed on the label – and the cat was out of the bag!*

Quite literally: cat's bile turned out to be a major source of flavouring.

18 June Even though we've been in Tuscany for less than a month, the people have already taught me so much about life. 'Slow down!' they say (or they would do, if they were capable of such brevity). 'Take time to stop and smell the rosemary.'

It's so easy to get caught up in the pace of modern living, isn't it? I shudder to think about my old routine back home. Up each morning, racing out the door, shopping, cleaning, dashing off to endorse a range of scented kitchen towelettes, then rushing back home again to throw something into the oven. What kind of an existence is that? We have to learn to draw breath. To relax and savour every moment. That said, the queue at the post office this morning was insufferably slow, exacerbated by the tendency of certain customers to turn the simplest of transactions into a lengthy social event. I'm all for catching up with local gossip, but not when a customer has been waiting *twenty-eight minutes* to pick up an important package from England.

While San Cisterno boasts many fine older style restaurants, not all cuisine here is strictly traditional. Places like Cucina Nuovella are doing some amazing things with molecular gastronomy. Guests at this two-star restaurant sit on furniture made out of actual food (terrines or baked meat). The crockery, too, is edible, unlike the food, which is largely decorative.

POLLO CON SALSA ACCIUGHE
CHICKEN WITH ANCHOVY SAUCE

I love this dish as a meal all by itself, or served with roughly torn chunks of crusty bread and a peppery salad, eaten from a tray while snuggled up in bed on crisp flannel sheets watching one of those musicals where a group of talented kids have to put on a show in order to save the town theatre from closing. But it can also be enjoyed as a casual mid-week supper when an old schoolfriend drops around with exciting news about finally being pregnant just when they thought IVF was the only option and you open a bottle of bubbly only she can't drink which is hilarious because she used to and you both get all silly. It's *that* versatile.

I × 1.5 KG CHICKEN, JOINTED

FRESHLY GROUND BLACK PEPPER, TO TASTE

I 1/2 TABLESPOONS OLIVE OIL

I SMALL ONION, FINELY CHOPPED

I CLOVE GARLIC, FINELY CHOPPED

125 ML DRY WHITE WINE

I 1/2 TABLESPOONS WHITE WINE VINEGAR

250 ML CHICKEN STOCK

1/2 TEASPOON DRIED OREGANO

I BAY LEAF

I TABLESPOON BLACK OLIVES, PITTED AND SLICED

3 ANCHOVY FILLETS, RINSED, DRIED AND CHOPPED

2 TABLESPOONS FRESH PARSLEY, CHOPPED

1. Wash the chicken under cold running water then pat dry with kitchen towel. Season with pepper.

2. Heat the olive oil in a heavy-based frying pan and cook the chicken, a few pieces at a time, until brown on both sides. Remove and set aside. Drain off the pan juices and discard.

3. Add the onion and garlic to the pan and cook, stirring incessantly, for 5 minutes until browned.

4. Stir in wine and vinegar, bring to the boil, then simmer until reduced.

5. Pour in the chicken stock and boil for 3 minutes.

6. Return the chicken pieces to the pan and add the oregano and bay leaf. Bring to the boil and simmer for 30 minutes until tender.

7. Remove the chicken pieces and set aside to keep warm. Remove the bay leaf and bring the stock to the boil, reducing until thickened.

8. Stir in the olives, anchovies and parsley and cook for another minute before pouring over the chicken.

AUDREY'S TIP

Most good butchers will joint a chicken for you on the spot. If unsure, I often ask a butcher to do it just as a test. If he can't, be prepared to exit the shop with as haughty an expression as you can muster.

19 June   When we first arrived at Villa del Vecchio, the garden, to put it mildly, was a disaster zone. Thick weeds, a tangle of stinging nettles, and everything covered in ivy.

As an environmentalist, I am passionately against the use of toxic herbicides, so Phillip and I did our best to tame this jungle by hand. As our only tools were a pair of secateurs and a bread knife, we eventually had to admit defeat, agreeing last week to try a small amount of weed killer. Called 'Ortobon', it came in a rather nasty-looking can with a large-breasted woman somewhat incongruously affixed to the label. We sprayed what we thought was a judicious amount onto some of the more impenetrable sections of our garden. It didn't seem to have any immediate effect but this morning we woke to a sea of dead vegetation: weeds, lawn, flower beds, the old apricot tree. Even sections of dry-stone wall appeared to be visibly crumbling. Naturally, we felt terrible and spent several hours attempting to replant as many sections as possible. It's certainly been a wake-up call.

Today we welcomed two more visitors to Villa del Vecchio: Gerald and Heather Weatherby. Like us, Gerald and Heather simply adore Tuscany and I thought a platter of local cheeses would make an ideal welcome. It turns out Heather is now lactose intolerant. She is also no longer eating gluten, which rules out any pasta or pastry dishes. To be perfectly honest, I think there's a fine line between food intolerance and simply being fussy.

Gerald and Heather enjoying the hospitality of our Tuscan garden. Gerald is an investigative journalist who has spent the past few years working on a biography of Jose Guadeca, the Peruvian human rights activist jailed for killing his wife – a crime he did not commit. After almost finishing this book Gerald was rocked by the news that Mr Guadeca had, in fact, confessed to the crime. It was a heartbreaking turn of events but all is not lost as Gerald tells us he may still be able to turn his work into a searing expose of a cold-hearted killer. Here's hoping.

"Many people think that making their own pastry is incredibly difficult and simply beyond them. It probably is."

20 June   With the weather now perfect, we have been taking the opportunity to eat most meals outdoors. Annoyingly, several pieces of garden furniture have now gone missing, so we've had to improvise a little. (The police say they know who's to blame and it's just a question of time before the culprits are apprehended.)

Gerald and Heather are certainly enjoying their stay with us. Heather loves to potter in the kitchen and describes herself as a 'self-taught cook', a phrase that for me instantly conjures up images of dirty fingernails and soggy risotto. Today she offered to help out with dinner and, while it was nice having some company in the kitchen, her attempts at zesting a lemon were – to put it kindly – hopeless. Bitter white pith throughout the peel. In the end I had to send her off to pick some parsley so I'd have a chance to throw everything out and start again.

I honestly can't think of a more perfect place to unwind at the end of a long summer's day than on our patio, beneath the branches of the old plum tree. It is here in this enchanting setting, surrounded by good friends and fine food, that one can truly appreciate a meal as more than just a means to an end, but as life itself. Which made the arrival of the wasps all the more disappointing. Phillip has tried spraying but this hasn't had much effect, so I guess we'll just have to get used to it.

21 June   Sad news from home that Sardi's, a restaurant we used to visit quite often back in London, has run into financial difficulties and been forced to close. While the food industry can be pretty cut-throat, no one likes to see a restaurant (even a rival one) fail. It's heartbreaking for all involved, especially the staff, who are suddenly out of a job. Then, of course, there's the poor owner, who is faced with the difficult choice of picking up the pieces and starting all over again with another restaurant venture, or giving up and becoming a food critic.

The Weatherbys have certainly settled into holiday life here at Villa del Vecchio. We enjoyed a sumptuous banquet outside this evening, the highlight being the artichoke and salami pizza, cooked to perfection in Phillip's wood-fired oven. Gerald certainly loved it, reaching for seconds, thirds and (not that I was counting) fifths before finally moving on to the cheese platter. Unfortunately, Heather had to head for bed early with what she described as a 'migraine', although I suspect it was little more than a mild headache from too much chianti.

MINESTRA DI RAPE, PATATE E FAGIOLI
RAPINI, POTATO AND BEAN SOUP

This simple soup used to be a staple on our entrée menu at audrey's. So much so that one food critic actually had the temerity to accuse us of being 'lazy'! (Not bad, coming from a writer who then went on to release a book made up entirely of his previous columns as if it was some sort of grandly original work instead of a hastily cobbled-together Christmas re-hash of ill-informed articles that no one even wanted to read in the first place.)

I CUP DRIED RED KIDNEY BEANS

I BUNCH RAPINI

3 MEDIUM POTATOES

EXTRA-VIRGIN OLIVE OIL

2 TABLESPOONS FINELY CHOPPED GARLIC

SEA SALT

FRESHLY GROUND BLACK PEPPER

1. If you are using dried beans, soak them overnight or for at least 6 hours. If you are using canned beans, stop right here and try something simpler.

2. Cut and peel the rapini, then wash in cold water. Bring a litre of water to the boil and blanch the rapini for 5–8 minutes or until tender. Retrieve the rapini, reserving the water, and finely chop.

3. Boil the unpeeled potatoes until tender.

4. In a frying pan, heat some olive oil and cook the garlic until a pale golden colour. Add the chopped rapini, and cook for another 10 minutes.

5. Add the drained beans and cook for a further 10 minutes, turning them occasionally.

6. When the potatoes are cooked, drain and peel them, then add to the rapini. Mash the potatoes as you cook, before pouring in the reserved water, stirring. Add as much water as you need to obtain the desired consistency.

7. Season with salt and pepper and serve.

AUDREY'S TIP

Do not be tempted to skip the blanching step and proceed directly to the sautéing, as blanched rapini will cook more completely and taste sweeter. Of course, if you don't believe me then go ahead and try it for yourself but don't say you weren't warned.

More of Audrey's dinner party etiquette

Ambience

When planning a dinner party, remember that low lighting can establish an intimate mood. It also negates the need to dust.

RSVPs

Most invitations will ask that you RSVP. When it comes to doing this, timing is all important. Too soon, and you risk coming across as unacceptably grateful. I prefer to hold off for at least a few weeks before giving a *provisional* acceptance (subject to shifting several other pressing social engagements), followed by a definite, formal confirmation the night before.

Dress code

Often guests you have invited to a function will phone and ask 'is there a dress standard?' My response at this point is to tell them that the event has been cancelled.

Setting the mood

Lighting, music and decoration are all important. I've been to dinner parties where my friends have gone to great lengths to transform their otherwise pedestrian houses into something quite appealing. Calico draped from the ceiling or tulle gathered and scalloped around a table can mask myriad home furnishing inadequacies.

Cancellations

No matter how carefully you plan a guest list, there will always be someone who insists on dropping out at the very last minute, throwing your seating arrangements into complete disarray. And, while there are some legitimate excuses (a bereavement or motor vehicle accident), I do not include illness as one of these. Headaches, flu, cramps, gastrointestinal distress – such minor indispositions all point to one thing: that your guest is placing their own personal comfort ahead of yours. Naturally, there's not much you can do at the time but I keep a list of invitees who have cancelled and make sure they are not given the opportunity to do so again at my expense.

Timing

'8.00 for 8.30pm' means what it says - that to be noticed you should arrive no earlier than 9.15pm.

22 June   I received an awkward email from a friend and fellow chef back home who is about to release her first cookbook and wants me to provide a quote for the front cover. This request created the most dreadful dilemma as I naturally want to be supportive but, to be honest, the book is not all that deserving of praise. In the end I opted for 'Good reliable recipes in an easy-to-read font', which should hopefully keep her happy while sending a suitably half-hearted endorsement.

The house is proving difficult to keep clean, especially with extra guests coming through, so we've got some hired help in. Her name is Slobodana, she's Romanian but seems quite trustworthy. Naturally we don't leave cash or jewellery lying around (there's no point in tempting fate, is there?) but she seems quite hardworking and reliable giving me time to get on with more important things.

ROTOLO DI VITELLO CON SEDANO E COUS COUS
VEAL ROLLS WITH CELERY AND COUSCOUS

Before attempting a complicated recipe for the first time it's often worth having a few practice runs. I know some chefs who like to test out new dishes at their local retirement village but personally I find it hard to get meaningful feed-back from diners who have only sampled your meal in pureed form.

4 LONG STICKS CELERY

12 SMALL, VERY THIN SLICES VEAL

FLOUR, FOR DUSTING

OLIVE OIL

100 ML WHITE WINE

1.5 LITRES GOOD STOCK

SALT

FRESHLY GROUND BLACK PEPPER

2 CUPS COUSCOUS

1. Slice the celery to make 12 small sticks.

2. Roll the veal around the celery and secure with a toothpick. Lightly dust with flour.

3. Heat olive oil in a frying pan and fry the veal rolls for a few minutes until they're just starting to brown.

4. Add the white wine and continue to cook for a few more minutes before adding the stock.

5. Season with salt and pepper and then simmer for 40 minutes. This should give you just enough time to find another plumber in the phonebook and arrange for the job to be completed properly once and for all.

6. Shortly before serving, prepare your couscous and spoon a generous amount onto each plate, followed by the veal.

AUDREY'S TIP

While the meat can be prepared well in advance, the couscous needs to be made at the last minute. If you don't own a *couscoussier* (it's hard to believe, but some people still don't!), just heat the grains above boiling water in an ordinary vegetable steamer and hope for the best.

23 June I simply love wandering through the markets here. At one cheese stall, the owner, Signor Ribolo, took me by the hand and carefully explained the difference between hard and soft, aged and fresh, sheep and cow. He was so generous and informative, wanting to help me make the right choice, that I simply couldn't bring myself to tell him that I'd already bought my cheese at the supermarket (it's so much cheaper and the range is surprisingly good). I still made a point of pretending to sample his wares and promised to come back next week.

The Weatherbys left this afternoon and I must say it is nice to have the house back to ourselves. Not that they weren't the most delightful of guests, but there's something about having your own space, isn't there? We've also had a breakthrough with our hot water system. A very efficient Czech gentleman by the name of Miroslava Svoboda (it was painted on the side of his van) responded promptly to my call and had the problem fixed within a couple of hours. To celebrate, I prepared the most decadent strawberry daiquiri and climbed into a deliciously warm bath. *Aaah!*

To market, to market!

'For me, there is no distinction between the cooking and the cook. The experience and passion of the person making the dish goes into the food, and so, in this way, the cook becomes part of the recipe. When you are eating my food, you are eating a part of me. It's a lovely thought, isn't it?'

24 June This morning we headed south to the village of Fortuna, where Phillip and I had booked to stay the weekend at a delightful *agriturismo* called Fattoria Chino.

We were greeted at the door by the farm's owner, Marga Gambara, who wasted no time in showing us around her ancient family home. Built in the seventeenth century, each room of the main farmhouse was decorated with a photo of Marga's late husband, except for the lounge, which instead housed a large urn containing his ashes.

The estate also included several outbuildings, such as a barn and wine cellar, along with a crumbling stone shed covered in weeds and overrun by stray cats. This turned out to be our room. Look, I'm all for rustic charm, but I feel that if you're going to run a tourist venture, there are basic standards to be observed.

Marga encourages her guests to get involved in the day-to-day activities of the farm and in no time Phillip and I found ourselves helping to make goat's milk cheese. After this Marga had us accompany her to the local markets to select fish and vegetables for that evening's meal. It was then back to the kitchen for some serious slicing, dicing, rolling and stuffing. After lunch we took another trip into town, this time to pick up Marga's dry cleaning, at which point we felt we'd had enough authentic rural experiences for one day.

Fattoria Chino, our home for the weekend.

BRUSCHETTA AL POMODORO
TOMATO BRUSCHETTA

Bruschetta would have to be Italy's quintessential summer appetiser. And what could be simpler than toasted bread, juicily ripe tomatoes, freshly picked basil and olive oil? One thing I cannot stress too highly is the importance of using good-quality olive oil. It lies at the heart of all great dishes, and there's simply no substitute. If you're not sure of the quality of your olive oil, pour a little into a bowl and inhale. Does it smell of freshly mown lawn on a wistful September afternoon with just a hint of rain in the air and the possibility of old schoolfriends dropping around for supper? No? Then put it back on the shelf.

4 VERY RIPE TOMATOES

2 TABLESPOONS EXTRA-VIRGIN OLIVE OIL

GOOD RED-WINE VINEGAR (OPTIONAL)*

HANDFUL FRESH BASIL LEAVES, ROUGHLY TORN
   INTO SMALL PIECES

SALT

FRESHLY GROUND BLACK PEPPER

4 SLICES SOURDOUGH BREAD

3 CLOVES GARLIC, 2 HALVED AND I ESPALIERED

Actually, it's not optional and you leave it out at your own peril.

1. Cut the tomatoes into 1 cm dice using a sharp knife and, if necessary, a measuring tape. Moisten with olive oil and vinegar, then add the basil, salt and pepper and leave for 30 minutes or half an hour, whichever comes first.

2. Grill thick slices of bread under a preheated grill or in a preheated griddle pan (for a truly authentic flavour, toast on an open fire), then rub the hot toast with a cut clove of garlic. This can be done sparingly if you prefer a subtle flavour, or generously if you like garlic and are not planning any form of close social interaction for the next few days.

3. Drizzle with olive oil then pile the tomato mixture generously onto the toast – it's not *bruschetta* if at least one guest doesn't end up with half of it on their shirt!

AUDREY'S TIP
Bruschetta is pronounced *brusketta*, not *brooshetta* as so many waiters back home laughably insist on calling it. When faced with such appalling ignorance the best option is to simply leave the restaurant or – at very least - reduce the size of your tip.

25 June

Up early to help with a few more chores on the farm. Despite being a city girl at heart, I can certainly see the charm of rural living. The pace of farm life here is slow, and totally in sync with the seasons. In spring, crops are planted. Late summer and autumn is harvest time. In winter, the fields lie fallow while agricultural subsidies are applied for.

The rest of the day was spent in Marga's kitchen, helping her make bread. Like me, Marga loves food and boasts an enormous knowledge of local cuisine. This afternoon she showed me a magnificent old cookbook that originally belonged to her great-grandmother. According to Marga, the book dated back to the eighteenth century, an assertion I didn't want to question despite the fact it contained several references to 'microwaves' and 'Tupperware'.

Marga's kitchen was typically Tuscan, boasting large cupboards, deep copper sinks, a wood stove and spiders.

The Black Plague reached Italy during the late fourteenth century and Tuscany was certainly not spared. The disease struck San Cisterno in 1348, choking its graveyards with bilious corpses, unleashing macabre religious cults, paralysing trade and forcing the cancellation of the city's annual Food and Wine Festival.

'Muffins are so popular and easy to prepare. I suspect that's why I hate them.'

26 June   A disappointing end to our trip away. When we returned home, we discovered we'd been broken into again. Luckily, the thieves were disturbed by Mariella, who was just going to bed when she heard noises from next door. No doubt the sight of a 76-year-old grandmother in her nightgown was enough to frighten them off, hopefully for good. The police say they've got a pretty good idea who was responsible (itinerant Polish labourers) and that it's just a question of time before they're apprehended.

On a happier note, we are now the proud owners of two ducks! Muddles and Maude (as we've nicknamed them!) must have arrived while we were away and have taken up residence outside our back door. Hopefully, we'll have fresh eggs any day now.

27 June   Summer has truly sprung here at Villa del Vecchio. The first cherries are making their appearance, bringing with them happy memories of childhood holidays in Devon when we would stay with my Uncle David and his second wife Maisie, who suffered dreadfully from migraines and insisted that we make no noise and refrain from touching any of the good furniture, meaning that we spent much of the day sitting in our cramped bedroom, too frightened to even step outside. Come to think of it, they were terrible times but the cherries made things a little more bearable.

I tell you what, Maude and Muddles have wasted no time settling in and we've really become quite fond of our 'girls'. Each day when we go outside they are there to greet us and can be heard chattering away. We're yet to find any eggs but Maude is definitely looking quite broody.

LINGUINE CON LE COZZE
MUSSEL LINGUINE

Mussels are a much underrated form of seafood. Our local fishmonger, Signora Ficinni, gets them in fresh each week. Remember, mussels need to be washed and then de-bearded before serving (two processes Signora Ficinni would do well to consider), and make sure to discard any that don't open when cooked.

300 G LINGUINE

OLIVE OIL

I CLOVE GARLIC, SLICED

PINCH OF DRIED CHILLI

2 RIPE TOMATOES, CHOPPED

GOOD HANDFUL MUSSELS,
   WASHED AND DE-BEARDED

HANDFUL CHOPPED PARSLEY

SALT

1. Bring a large pot of salted water to the boil and add the linguine.

2. While this is cooking, heat some olive oil in a pan and add the garlic and a pinch of dried chilli.

3. As the garlic begins to cook, add the chopped tomatoes.

4. Add the mussels, give the pan a toss and place the lid on until all the mussels have opened. At this point you can add a handful of chopped parsley.

5. By now the linguine should be cooked, so drain the water, put the pasta back in the pot and stir in the mussel sauce.

6. Allow it to cook for another minute, drizzle on a little more olive oil, season and serve.

AUDREY'S TIP

Fresh seafood will not smell. When shopping, ask your fishmonger what time the catch came in. He'll probably lie, so don't hesitate to ask for proof. Be on the lookout for pale eyes and a fishy smell. If you detect these (in either the produce or proprietor), consider shopping elsewhere.

'It's such a shame that people no longer take
the time to sit and enjoy a leisurely, healthy breakfast.
I would rank the demise of the traditional breakfast as one
of the greatest tragedies of the past century, up there with
global warming, nuclear proliferation and those little
stickers you get on apples. All so unnecessary!'

28 June It's been over two weeks since the Sandersons left. Yet, disappointingly, we have still not received a thank you card. Of course, they presented us with a small gift basket but I hardly feel that a few scented soaps (bulked out with a *lot* of raffia) can fully make up for a formal, written acknowledgement.

I found some wonderful tomatoes at the *supermercato* this morning, plump and oozingly ripe, only to discover that they were actually from Spain. Naturally, I was appalled (determined as I am to eat only local produce) but they were so cheap I just had to grab a small basketful. I bought some Italian parsley to 'balance' things out.

29 June Well, it's been a glorious week of clear blue skies and sun. For those of you suffering through another lacklustre English summer, all I can say is sorry!

To celebrate this perfect weather we decided to go on a picnic. I love picnics. What could be better than cooking up lashings of scrumptious food, driving somewhere else, and then eating it in a slightly less comfortable setting?

First we headed into town for provisions. Somehow our combination of mime and mangled Italian got us pretty much everything we needed: fresh bread, cheese, olives and prosciutto, along with a packet of condoms (Phillip was actually attempting to indicate he wanted a small salami). Then it was into the car and away we went.

The picnic itself was a little disappointing. For a start, the field we planned on using had just been ploughed and was now covered in a layer of rather pungent fertiliser. By the time we drove to a more suitable location, the marinated olives were starting to leak over the cheese and Phillip realised that he'd forgotten the pepper grinder. Ants were another unwelcome intrusion and we ended up having to finish our cheese platter in the car. But you know what? It still tasted wonderful and was well worth the effort.

'For me, dessert should be more than just the last course of a meal. It's the culinary climax and, as such, I want it to represent a shuddering, earth-shaking release, a palate-pounding explosion of tastes and textures that leaves one both energised and alive yet with a hint of drained, melancholic languor. Or you can just have cheese.'

TORTA DI CILIEGIE
CHERRY PIE

The market was selling such luscious ripe cherries this week that I simply had to do something with them. There is a wonderful sense of anticipation, coupled with comforting familiarity, when you cook with the seasons. What's more, failure to do so has been linked to all sorts of modern maladies, from depression and diabetes to illiteracy and increased divorce rates.

25 G UNSALTED BUTTER, MELTED

CASTER SUGAR

400 G CHERRIES

200 G PLAIN FLOUR

1/2 TEASPOON BAKING POWDER

PINCH OF SALT

300 ML MILK

250 ML CREAM

6 FREE-RANGE EGGS

I TEASPOON PURE VANILLA EXTRACT

ICING SUGAR, TO DUST

DOUBLE CREAM, TO SERVE

1. Preheat oven to 200ºC.

2. Brush a shallow baking dish with melted butter and sprinkle a tablespoon of caster sugar over the dish to evenly coat it. Wash the cherries and set aside.

3. Sift the flour, baking powder and salt into a bowl and mix well, then add 300 g caster sugar.

4. In another bowl, whisk the milk, cream, eggs and vanilla extract. Slowly add this mixture to the flour, stirring to create a smooth batter.

5. Arrange the cherries over the base of the prepared dish and pour the batter over the top. Bake for 25–30 minutes until golden and firm.

6. Dust with icing sugar and serve immediately, with a dollop of extra thick double cream!

AUDREY'S TIP

When cooking with cherries I like to leave the stones in, as removing them means you lose juice. However, there's always someone who will manage to chip a tooth or, worse, ruin your dinner by starting to choke. When serving this dish at audrey's our staff were warned to be on stand-by, ready to deliver the Heimlich manoeuvre, followed by a distracting bowl of complimentary chocolates.

30 June Somewhat disturbing news today regarding our ducks. It turns out Maude is actually a boy. Our neighbour Paolo made the discovery (I don't dare enquire how) but it certainly explains his rather aggressive behaviour. Meanwhile, Muddles has become quite territorial, pecking and clacking her beak at anyone who attempts to walk out the back door. They're also both leaving a great mess on the patio and, with no eggs produced so far, I'm not sure we can really keep them for much longer.

This evening we sampled another local restaurant, Rinaldo, that had been highly recommended. The food was excellent and the staff certainly attentive. Even the owner made an appearance later in the evening, wandering from table to table in a bright gold dress and matching sandals, asking patrons if they were having a good time. (We subsequently found out that this woman wasn't the owner, just a regular patron with some sort of mental disorder, but she still added a colourful touch.)

Rinaldo, *another of San Cisterno's delightful restaurants.*

Arriving back at the house we were almost set upon by Maude and Muddles, who greeted us with a great deal of fierce quacking and flapping of wings. We'll really have to think of something to do with this troublesome pair.

PAPARO ALL'ARANCIA
DUCK WITH ORANGE

In our mad, frantic lives, few people have time for fiddly or complicated meals. (Which could well explain the poor sales of my third book, *Audrey's Fiddly & Complicated Meals*.) However, this dish is worth the extra effort and, after one or two practice runs, I think you'll find it quite achievable.

1. Pre-heat oven to 190°C.

2. Wash and dry the duck. Place the garlic, rosemary, salt, pepper and zest of 1 orange into the cavity.

3. Pour a good glug of olive oil into a large roasting pan. Add the duck, surround the bird with vegetables, add another glug of oil over everything. Roast for about 1½ hours. Ten minutes into the roasting time, pour the wine over the duck.

4. Peel the zest from the remaining 2 oranges and cut into very thin strips. Peel and halve the pears. Place oranges and pears in a saucepan with 750ml water and bring to the boil, then drain. Repeat the process two more times in order to remove the bitterness.

5. Half an hour into the roasting time, squeeze the juice from the 2 oranges and pears over the duck.

6. Heat the sugar, 2 tablespoons water and the lemon juice over a low heat until the sugar caramelises. Add the strips of orange zest and continue to cook, stirring, for 2 minutes, then set aside.

7. When the duck is cooked, remove the garlic, rosemary and orange zest from the cavity. Transfer the meal to a baking dish, then spoon over the caramelised orange zest. Return to the oven for a further 10 minutes. Serve hot.

I × 1.2 KG DUCK

I CLOVE GARLIC

SPRIG OF ROSEMARY

SALT

FRESHLY GROUND
   BLACK PEPPER

3 ORANGES

3 PEARS

EXTRA-VIRGIN OLIVE OIL

I CARROT, COARSELY CHOPPED

I ONION, ROUGHLY CHOPPED

I STICK CELERY, GENTLY
   CHOPPED

250 ML DRY WHITE WINE

½ CUP SUGAR

750 ML WATER

2 TABLESPOONS WATER

I TABLESPOON LEMON JUICE

AUDREY'S TIP

Take care when heating the sugar; you want it to melt slowly and turn a lovely golden brown. If it burns, you've heated it too quickly and should probably move on to a less challenging recipe. (There are some lovely simple salads in this book.)

Luglio
july

I July

I love markets. Not the touristy belts-and-baubles kind, but genuine food markets such as the one we have in San Cisterno. People who shop at markets care about their food. They want to squeeze their plums, sniff their fish, prod their poultry and, most importantly, *connect* with the person selling it. A market stallholder will have very definite ideas about the best way of cooking their produce. These ideas are often wrong but nonetheless firmly held. And it's not just the quality of what's being sold. Even the courtesy and personal attention is something to be savoured. *'Buongiorno, signora, come sta?'* I still tingle every time I hear this. The closest many of us get to a social exchange in the supermarket is *'Any cash out?'* Give me markets any day.

The house behind us is occupied by Alphonse 'Nonno' Giancardi. Nonno is eighty-six but he continues to live at home, cooking and cleaning for himself. What's more, he still has an eye for the ladies (a tendency currently being kept in check via regular medication). For weeks now we've been meaning to invite Alphonse over for lunch and today seemed like the perfect opportunity. The Pasquinis also joined us for a delightfully relaxing afternoon. Dining with Italian friends is quite an experience. They eat with such gusto, it's a joy to behold. And meals are made to be lingered over. In some parts of Tuscany the traditional Sunday lunch quite often extends until well after dark on Tuesday. *La dolce vita!*

Despite his age, Nonno still chops his own wood, trims the grapevines and, on Sunday afternoons, even goes rabbit shooting. During this period we've been advised to either stay indoors or wear something bright and bullet-proof.

'For me, cooking is always a process of discovery. When holding a carrot, I often find myself thinking, "What's something truly special I can do with this? Slice and steam it? Or grate it and serve it raw? What if I kept the peel on? Or perhaps added more peel, but from another vegetable? What if the carrot was julienned and not eaten, merely used as garnish?" It's an exciting mental journey I go on every time I step into the kitchen. The only downside is that making a cup of tea can sometimes take over an hour.'

2 July Up early for some serious work in the garden. The combination of warm weather and recent rainfall has meant that the weeds are literally bursting out of the ground. Our vegetable patch is in excellent shape and I'm looking forward to sampling some home-grown produce, free from pesticides and other nasties. There is no argument that there is a clear connection between good food and organic food. I've actually read of hospitals in America that have stopped prescribing antibiotics and are instead treating patients with infusions of organic vegetables and macrobiotic poultices. Of course, the medical experts are sceptical but it's only a matter of time before these sorts of approaches really take off.

3 July Our dear friends Lynne and Victor Siddle arrived today, and told us of a most unpleasant experience they had a few days ago in Florence when some gypsies tried to steal their bags. Apparently, they were just coming out of their hotel when a shabbily dressed woman approached them and literally threw her young child at Lynne, no doubt in an attempt to distract her. Luckily for all concerned, Lynne does not particularly care for children and she let the baby drop to the ground (while keeping both hands *firmly* on her camera). Even so, it was a close shave for all concerned. We assured them there would be no such incidents here in sleepy San Cisterno!

   After dinner we sat out on the vine-covered terrace beneath a canopy of shining stars, the shimmering moonlight illuminating the silver leaves of the olive grove stretching away in front of us. In such an idyllic setting, it was hard to imagine wanting for anything else. Some insect repellent, perhaps, as the local mosquito population has turned out to be both large and determined.

TORTA ALLE NOCCIOLE E CIOCCOLATO
CHOCOLATE AND HAZELNUT CAKE

When this recipe first appeared in my book *Divine Desserts*, we made the most terrible mix-up with the instructions (of course, when I say 'we', the fault lay firmly at the feet of the junior editor). Instead of reading 'microwave for 30 seconds' it read 'microwave for 30 *minutes*', meaning that many of my readers were setting off smoke alarms and wasting perfectly good organic chocolate. Naturally, we published a correction in the second edition but this didn't stop some opportunists attempting to sue me for all sorts of imagined ill effects, from cracked bowls to post-traumatic stress disorder. Needless to say, we've double-checked the instructions this time.

400 G HAZELNUTS

400 G DARK CHOCOLATE

400 G UNSALTED BUTTER, SOFTENED,
   AT ROOM TEMPERATURE

300 G CASTER SUGAR

PINCH OF SALT

10 ORGANIC EGGS

1. Preheat oven to 160°C.

2. Place the hazelnuts in a frying pan and roast them over a low heat until they are just starting to colour; take care not to burn them. To remove the skins, put the hazelnuts in a clean tea towel, fold the towel over and rub between your hands. Place the nuts in a food processor and pulse to coarsely grind.

3. Place the chocolate in a double-boiler and let it melt. Remove and allow to cool slightly.

4. In a bowl, beat the soft butter with the sugar and salt until light and fluffy. Add the melted chocolate, blending well.

5. Add 1 egg at a time to the mixture until all are well combined. Gently fold in the ground hazelnuts.

6. Pour the mixture into a buttered 28 cm cake tin and bake for about 40 minutes.

7. When cooked, open the oven door and turn off the heat, leaving the cake in the oven to cool for another 30 minutes.

AUDREY'S TIP

If you are going to attempt this cake, it is absolutely essential that you use the finest quality chocolate. If unsure, look for dark, single-plantation, organic varieties with a cocoa butter content of at least 70 per cent. As a rule, anything coated in peanuts or coconut can safely be ruled out.

More of Audrey's dinner party etiquette

Welcome

After greeting your guests, it's considerate to offer them somewhere to leave their belongings and a chance to 'brush up' (or apply deodorant, as required).

Gifts

As they arrive, some guests may present you with chocolates, a bottle of wine or other small gifts. These should be placed aside and later thrown out. If the gift is food, some guests will expect it to be served as part of the event. This is short-sighted and quite unreasonable. If I have carefully planned dessert as a pavé of lime served with fresh seasonal berries, then the addition of chocolate nougat (handmade or otherwise) is going to do nothing but upset the delicate flavour balance and clutter the table.

Punctuality

If certain guests phone to say they are running late, assure them it's not a problem and then hold off serving anyone else until the main course is slightly burnt. This way your latecomers will realise that their lack of punctuality has not only caused everyone to wait but has also *ruined* the meal. Hopefully, they'll be sufficiently mortified to arrive on time in future, should you be magnanimous enough to invite them.

Introductions

On many occasions, you will have invited guests who do not know each other. In these instances, a clearly spoken and simple introduction is called for, often with a small conversation starter such as, 'This is Leanne Powlett, whose husband has just left her for a Czech girl half his age,' or 'Allow me to present Aiden Coombes and his homosexual partner, Carl.' Then you can go and check the *canapés*, safe in the knowledge that your guests now have something to talk about.

Name tags

Under no circumstances should name tags be used. While these may be appropriate for office parties or charity functions, guests in a private home do not wish to have labels attached to them and I for one will simply refuse to wear a sticker, badge or lanyard.

Comfort

Be sensitive to your guests' enjoyment. Some people are frightened of dogs, allergic to cats, or simply prefer not to have elderly people in view. Make sure all such potential hazards are suitably restrained before anyone arrives.

4 July

Oh dear. I woke to a rather 'pointed' email from my publisher. Apparently, we've exceeded our photography budget again. Oops! I sent a reply, making all the appropriate noises and promising to be more selective over the coming weeks. But this place is just so visually stunning! Every olive grove, vineyard, terracotta roof – even the crockery – just screams out to be captured on film.

Our guests Lynne and Victor have both truly settled in. We told them to 'treat the place like their own', an offer that's been accepted perhaps just a touch too literally. I found several wet towels lying in the bathroom this morning and a half-full mug of tea left on the hall table without a coaster. After lunch, Victor asked if he could play one of his jazz CDs; naturally we said yes, not realising there'd be piercing trumpet blasting through the house for the next two hours. Still, it was delightful to see them so relaxed, even if this was at the expense of others.

Our dear friends Lynne and Victor enjoying an evening meal at Villa del Vecchio.

ZUPPA DI PESCE
FISH SOUP

While lobsters should be purchased alive to ensure freshness, killing them humanely is important. There are several options. I prefer to place them humanely in the freezer for half an hour or so. Another method is 'drowning' them humanely in fresh water (Perrier works well) or humanely running a knife through their brain. To be honest, it really doesn't matter what you do, provided the word 'humanely' is used.

1. After killing the lobsters, remove the tails and set aside. Cut the heads open. Inside you will find a grey sac which is best discarded. Chop into pieces.

2. Heat a few glugs of olive oil in a large pot and add the pieces of lobster head. Throw in the onion, garlic, carrot and chillies and cook for about 15 minutes until the onion starts to colour.

3. Add the white wine and tomatoes, and turn up the heat to boil for a good 10 minutes. You can add a few cups of water if things start to dry out.

4. Place a colander on top of another pot and strain the broth through it, pressing down on the shells with a spoon to extract as much liquid as possible. Once all the liquid has drained (I like to leave it to drip for 5 minutes or so), put the broth on a low heat to simmer.

5. Slice the lobster tails into small chunks and place in the broth. Crack open the claws and add the meat to the broth. Layer mussels over the top and allow to cook for 10 minutes.

7. Add the dried lasagne fragments and cook for another 10 minutes.

8. Season well and serve hot.

2 × 1 KG LIVE LOBSTERS

20 MUSSELS IN SHELLS

500 G WHITE FLESHY FISH

EXTRA-VIRGIN OLIVE OIL

1 ONION, FINELY CHOPPED

5 CLOVES GARLIC, FINELY CHOPPED

1 CARROT, PEELED AND FINELY CHOPPED

2 SMALL DRIED RED CHILLIES

375 ML DRY WHITE WINE

1 KG TOMATOES, PEELED AND CHOPPED

200 G SMALL & BROKEN DRIED LASAGNE SHEETS

SEA SALT & FRESHLY GROUND BLACK PEPPER

AUDREY'S TIP

While the kindest way to 'dispatch' a lobster is to place it in the freezer for half an hour before cooking, if you're pushed for time (or simply feeling angry) a metal skewer between the eyes will do the trick. I wouldn't recommend reversing the car over one, unless you're planning seafood patties.

5 July

The plan was to head off early for some sightseeing this morning but by 10.45 am Lynne and Victor had yet to emerge from their room. I didn't want to knock, but in the end I was forced to get out the Hoover as we had a 12.30 luncheon reservation in the nearby village of Tussino.

The main attraction is the town's magnificent sixteenth-century cathedral, and we were lucky enough to be given a guided tour by one of its resident monks, ending in a climb up into the bell tower where he promised 'a view we would never forget'. This claim was fully realised when a gust of wind lifted our guide's cassock into the air, revealing little in the way of undergarments.

Lunch was at a small bistro called Casa Luna, and the food was excellent. I had a simple salad of artichokes dressed in oil and white balsamic vinegar, which is something of a speciality in this part of Italy, although Lynne claimed she had seen the same brand of vinegar for sale back home at Tesco. I don't think so! For dessert we all shared a tasting plate of delicate regional pastries, however Phillip was being careful as his cholesterol levels are starting to creep up again, so he stuck to cheese.

6 July

It turns out Lynne was right about the vinegar, it is now sold at Tesco. And more cheaply than here in Tuscany, which is somewhat disappointing. I've ordered some online but it won't be here for another week or so.

I spent a busy morning in the kitchen, preparing our evening meal. Lynne woke late and offered to help, although – typically – by this stage most of the work had been done. I got her to wash a few dishes but that went badly when she accidentally knocked over and broke my favourite salad bowl. Naturally, she felt terrible and blamed herself. So did I, but of course I didn't say anything.

"I want my food to reflect how we eat today: shared plates, no plates, plates of different sizes or shapes, plates that look like plates but are actually bowls — the possibilities are as endless as they are exciting."

TV TIMES

Despite my years spent running some of the finest restaurants in London, not to mention writing numerous award-winning books and regular newspaper columns, I have to accept that a large number of food-lovers know me best through my long-running television series *Audrey's Kitchen*. Ground-breaking for its time (we were the first to put a camera inside the cavity of a chicken), *Audrey's Kitchen* pioneered techniques and ideas that are still being slavishly copied to this day by so-called 'celebrity chefs'.

I think what people most loved about *Audrey's Kitchen* was its sense of authenticity. Everything we showed was real. Of course, the programme wasn't shot in my actual kitchen – we had a replica built – and some of the dishes had to be pre-prepared so we could do the close-ups in one go, but the techniques I demonstrated were both simple and genuine.

Naturally, things didn't always go to plan! I remember for one episode we wanted to film a sequence where I serve a casual meal to a group of friends who have dropped by unexpectedly. We had organised for some of my actual friends to take part but several decided to pull out at the last minute (which, if you don't mind me saying so, is just typical), so we were forced to use extras who were, quite simply, a bunch of idiots. One even attempted to eat an entrée before we'd got the close-ups done, which very nearly proved disastrous. To make matters even more complicated, it turned out I was not allowed to speak directly to these people (union rules stipulate that extras must be directed by the floor manager), so every instruction had to be passed on like Chinese whispers. Really, you wouldn't think it would be that hard to simply sit at a table and pretend to be having a good time, but we ended up having to shoot most of them from behind and then dub in some laughter later on.

Then there were the times we shot on location, such as one episode at Grovewood Estate in Devon. Despite a howling wind and intermittent rain, our genius director still insisted on doing the cooking *al fresco*. The barbecue gas burner kept getting blown out and we had to weigh the tablecloth down with rocks and one of the lighting assistants. The glamour of television? I don't think so.

7 July

Could the weather be any more perfect? Calm, clear and – almost – too hot. Fortunately, the stone walls of Villa del Vecchio keep most of our rooms at a more than pleasant temperature. Victor and Lynne are having a wonderful time and spent the day exploring San Cisterno's many attractions. In terms of house guests, we're pretty casual and really only have one rule – that they enjoy themselves! Of course, we also insist on a certain standard of dress and general willingness to help out with chores around the villa, but these are hardly 'rules', merely reasonable expectations. Which makes the Siddles' behaviour today so much harder to understand. If you're going out for pre-dinner drinks, then that's exactly what they should be – *pre*-dinner. To wander in at 8.37 pm reeking of *Chianti* and then expect a perfectly cooked meal seems a little unreasonable in my book.

When we first moved in we discovered this large apricot tree at the rear of the property that, according to Mariella, had been there for over 70 years! We felt sad about having it chopped down but the leaves were simply playing havoc with our pool filter. And we cheered ourselves up by using the last of its fruit to make a luscious dessert

'Along with sex, cooking for someone would have to rank as one of the most fundamental acts of love. It's also one that, generally speaking, involves less washing up…'

8 July

One of the joys of escaping to Tuscany has been getting away from the dreadful British press and their interminable quest to find fault with those more talented or successful. So I should have known better than to read the article in the *Daily Mirror* forwarded to me by an insensitive colleague. It was ostensibly a piece about 'celebrity endorsements' but turned out to be little more than a thinly veiled attack on me and my decision to appear in a recent series of television commercials.

As usual, the article was full of gross inaccuracies ('selling out') and wild exaggeration (I was not paid anything like the £2 million quoted!), so let's just set the record straight, shall we? Agreeing to be the face of Kwik n' Easy™ Ready-Cooked Home-Style Frozen Meals was not a decision I entered into lightly. After years of passionately and tirelessly championing the importance of seasonal produce grown locally, it naturally took some convincing for me to lend my name to a product line that leaned so heavily on freeze-dried ingredients. But if you could have met with the makers, as I did, you would have understood that they shared the same love of fine dining that drives us all. Their head chef, in particular, was most inspiring, combining a passion for quality food with a master's degree in chemical engineering.

Unfortunately, the finished advertisements did not fully capture my strongly held views on the importance of food as both a nurturing and uniting force, one that reflects both who we are and how we feel about ourselves. But that's not an easy message to get across in thirty seconds, especially when you've got to leave room for the pack shot and dancing carrots. All I can say is please – no more news from home. I'm off to plant some basil.

One of the things I most treasure about asparagus is their ephemeral nature: the season runs from late spring to early summer; barely a blink of the eye and then they're gone! Unlike the Siddles, who have decided to stay on for an extra day.

RISOTTO AI FUNGHI ARROSTO CON PREZZEMOLO
ROASTED MUSHROOM RISOTTO WITH PARSLEY

When I cooked this risotto for supper it was simply devoured by our guests. In fact, Victor declared it to be the 'best risotto he had ever tasted!' Although Lynne was a little less effusive in her praise and ate very little. To be fair, she is watching her weight (and for good reason), yet she certainly enjoyed dessert, so it's hard to really be sure.

1 LITRE CHICKEN OR VEGETABLE STOCK

OLIVE OIL

BUTTER

I LARGE ONION, CHOPPED

2 CLOVES GARLIC, CHOPPED

2 CUPS ARBORIO RICE

SALT

200 G WILD MUSHROOMS

4 TABLESPOONS FRESHLY GRATED PARMESAN,
    PLUS EXTRA TO SERVE

I SMALL BUNCH FRESH FLAT-LEAF PARSLEY,
    LEAVES PICKED

I SMALL BUNCH FRESH THYME, LEAVES PICKED

JUICE OF I LEMON

1. Preheat oven to 200°C.

2. Heat the stock in a saucepan.

3. In a separate pan, heat 2 tablespoons of olive oil and a knob of butter. Add the onion and garlic, and cook slowly for about 15 minutes.

4. When the onion has softened, add the rice and turn up the heat. Keep stirring the rice to prevent it burning.

5. Add your first ladle of hot stock and a good pinch of salt. Turn the heat down and keep ladling in the stock, stirring the rice as each ladleful is absorbed.

6. Taste the rice to see if it's cooked; if not, add more stock. If you run out of stock before the rice is cooked, add some boiling water or consider eating out.

7. Pour a splash of olive oil into an oven pan. Add the mushrooms and place in the preheated oven to roast for 6 minutes or until cooked through.

8. Add a knob of butter and the grated parmesan to the rice and stir in the parsley and thyme.

9. Roughly chop half the roasted mushrooms and stir into the risotto, adding a good squeeze of lemon juice.

10. Divide between plates and sprinkle over the remaining mushrooms. Serve with grated parmesan.

AUDREY'S TIP

I often like to add some finely chopped minced pork to this dish, although if, like me, you have Jewish friends you can use beef or simply not invite them.

9 July

The Siddles left yesterday so we've finally got the house back to ourselves again. Phillip used the opportunity to get out his easel and paints while I spent much of the day pottering in the kitchen.

In the evening we treated ourselves to dinner in town at a newly opened *trattoria* recommended by the Pasquinis. To be honest, we were a little disappointed. My *linguine puttanesca* tasted far too salty. Meanwhile, Phillip had the twice-cooked duck, which he felt was slightly under-cooked. On top of this, a television had been left on in the kitchen and could be heard quite loudly throughout our meal. I realise it was an important football match but still, it could have at least been turned down.

I'm all for authentic dining experiences but to my mind there's a significant difference between 'rustic charm' and simply not changing your table linen.

10 July

There's high excitement here in San Cisterno today, with 10 July marking the town's *festa*, or 'feast day'. Italians love to celebrate special events, whether it's the commemoration of an ancient battle or the opening of a new tollway section. Festivities usually begin with a mass, followed by a street parade and market. The market turned out to be a little disappointing, with shopkeepers simply dragging their wares outside and selling them on plastic tables at somewhat inflated prices. Of course, this didn't stop the crowds flooding in to be part of the excitement, and tourists could be seen everywhere. Phillip and I now consider ourselves 'locals' and naturally found this invasion a little hard to take. The worst offenders would have to be the Japanese, who insist on pushing ahead in queues as if the fact that they are holding an expensive video camera gives them some sort of journalistic imperative. In the end we were forced to retreat to the sanctity of Villa del Vecchio, where we watched the fireworks display from our upstairs balcony.

'No matter how impoverished a country may be, I believe its people must have access to the basic necessities: food, clean drinking water and non-stick pans.'

MAIONESE

MAYONNAISE

Mayonnaise is the easiest of sauces to make, and I find it difficult to accept that it is ever really necessary to buy it ready-made. Perhaps if one were incapacitated by a sudden and catastrophic physical ailment that made it impossible to move even a single muscle and you suddenly realised that you had guests arriving in half an hour, then one might *consider* opening a store-bought variety – but even then I'd have serious reservations.

2 LARGE FREE-RANGE EGG YOLKS

1 TEASPOON DIJON MUSTARD

PINCH OF SEA SALT

250 ML EXTRA-VIRGIN OLIVE OIL

250 ML VEGETABLE OIL

1. The key to making mayonnaise is confidence. If you start thinking about all the things that might go wrong, you'll never even try. Begin by whisking the egg yolks, mustard and salt until thick.

2. Next, begin dripping in the oil, drop by drop, until it 'takes' and becomes thick. This is the most critical moment and requires your complete, 110 per cent concentration. Do NOT pour the oil in too quickly or the mixture will curdle. I'll say this again. In *italics*. And red. *Do NOT pour too quickly.* It is absolutely essential that you do not rush the process.

3. If you're patient, you should end up with a smooth, creamy mixture that will provide the perfect accompaniment to everything from chicken to salad. If you are not patient, you will end up with a coagulated mess.

AUDREY'S TIP

Should the mixture curdle, don't worry. This happens to just about all untrained cooks. Simply tip everything into a large plastic bag and hide all evidence of your failure in the bin. Then you can start again, or consider moving house.

11 July Today Phillip and I went in search of homemade goat's cheese. After making our way along a series of dusty tracks, we came upon an isolated farmhouse, in front of which sat an elderly couple. Whether husband and wife or brother and sister we weren't sure. (And, to be frank, in these smaller villages the two are not always mutually exclusive.) 'Yes,' they told us, they did have some cheese and we were ushered into a dimly lit kitchen cool room. Here we saw an ancient wooden bench, giant *prosciutti* stacked in a corner and festoons of tomatoes hanging from the roof, along with garlic, chillies and – somewhat disturbingly – the Signora's underwear. Honestly, we could have just stepped back to the nineteenth century, had it not been for the large plasma television mounted on the wall playing *Housewives Desperato*.

After selling us some wonderful-looking cheese, the owners were keen to show us around their humble farm. The woman (we never did catch her name) was understandably proud of her rambling vegetable garden, and insisted we pick some courgettes. Across from the house was a stone barn where, according to the husband, they kept the cows and chickens, as well as their youngest son Onofrio, who was, to use his description, 'sick in the head'. Next door was a pen for the goats, who looked happy and well fed. I assured them their cheese would be well used!

Our local cheese supplier!

'When it comes to food, one must always embrace change
regardless of risk. During the 1960s my uncle Bryan worked as
a chef at a pub in Newcastle. One night he decided to surprise
the regulars and instead of the normal steak sandwiches,
he served a warm salad made up of oakleaf, endive and shallots
with chicken livers sautéed in a sherry vinaigrette.
He was found two days later unconscious in a nearby laneway.'

12 July   In Tuscany, tradition is valued and maintained. How often in cities at home do we pass each other by without so much as a 'hello' or even a nod of recognition? Here, locals stop, shake hands, embrace. A kiss on each cheek is considered customary, with two kisses for those you know well and three for someone you love or owe money to.

Summer evenings are still celebrated with the *passeggiata*, a centuries-old tradition in which townsfolk parade around the centre of town dressed in their finery. The fact that this ritual is now more commonly performed in high-powered sports cars in no way diminishes its authentic charm.

Before buying any produce I always ask myself these questions: 'Where does it come from?' 'Is it fresh?' 'In season?' 'Grown locally?' 'Does it inspire me to cook?' 'Should I have put more coins in the parking meter?'

ZUPPA INGLESE CLASSICA
CLASSIC TRIFLE

This is another of my maternal grandmother's recipes, transcribed from one of her old kitchen diaries dating from the 1940s. I've changed it a little, simply replacing the glacé fruit and powdered eggs, and erasing several anti-German sentiments scrawled in the margins. I've also reduced the amount of cream sherry.

10 TRIFLE SPONGES

200 G BLACKCURRANT JAM

1 PACKET AMARETTI BISCUITS

250 ML SHERRY

JUICE OF $\frac{1}{2}$ LEMON

750 G BLACKBERRIES OR RASPBERRIES

2 EGGS, SEPARATED

100 G CASTER SUGAR

750 G MASCARPONE

50 G FLAKED ALMONDS, LIGHTLY TOASTED

1. Spread the trifle sponges with 100 g jam. Line the base of a glass bowl with the sponges.

2. Crumble the amaretti biscuits (the food processor works well for this) and scatter over the sponges. Pour 125 ml sherry over the top.

3. Heat the remaining jam in a saucepan with the lemon juice and add the berries. Once the berries have softened, pour the mixture into the sponge-lined bowl.

4. In another bowl, whisk the egg yolks with the caster sugar until smooth. Drip in the remaining 125 ml sherry, continuing to mix until light and frothy. Fold in the mascarpone and mix until smooth.

5. In a third bowl, whisk the egg whites until firm then fold into the mascarpone mixture. Spread the mixture over the berries in the glass bowl.

6. Cover the bowl and place in the fridge for a minimum of 2 hours; 4 hours is better.

7. When ready to serve, allow the trifle to return to room temperature before topping with the almonds.

AUDREY'S TIP

If good-quality mascarpone is unavailable, a mixture of one part *crème fraîche* and three parts double cream will make a suitably disappointing alternative.

13 July

For lunch today Phillip and I sampled some of the beautiful goat's cheese we'd bought a few days ago. I made a simple salad of figs and dill, over which we crumbled some feta-style raw milk cheese. *Mmm!*

Phillip's sister Helena arrived this afternoon for another stay. She says she 'misses her brother' and just had to come back to spend some more time with us. Funny, Helena only sees Phillip once or twice a year back in England, but now we're in Tuscany the familial bonds seem overwhelming. This time she's brought a new boyfriend, Ashley, and they certainly seem very happy together. Poor Helena has been desperately unlucky on the romance front over the years, so one can only hope that this relationship lasts longer than her previous ill-fated efforts at coupling. I'll certainly be doing my best to 'grease the wheels'.

'So much of what we feel about food comes from our parents. I only have to pick up a meat mallet to be reminded of my mother.'

14 July

Just to the east of San Cisterno lies one of the region's most famous wineries, Truilli Estate. Today we were invited by its owner, Mario Truilli, to visit and sample some of their latest vintage.

Mario's family has been producing wine here for over a hundred years. Their big breakthrough as winemakers came twenty-five years ago when Mario's father, Franco, began using grapes instead of artichokes, greatly expanding his potential market.

After arriving at the main house, Mario kindly offered to show us around his winery. Our tour started in the estate's cellar shop, where Phillip and I felt somewhat obliged to purchase a few bottles. After this we headed into the bottling plant, where head winemaker Giacomo Fusilli explained his passion for the process of winemaking. 'I have a mistress – she is the grapevine!' he laughingly told us. (Although it subsequently turned out that Signor Fusilli did in fact have a mistress, a young girl who was working in the estate's marketing department.)

TRUILLI ESTATE
Now specialising in chianti-style wines, Truilli remains a small boutique winery, producing just 10,000 bottles a year. Believe it or not, this entire vintage is sold and consumed within San Cisterno, much of it by the one family.

SALTIMBOCCA ALLA ROMANA
VEAL WITH PROSCIUTTO AND SAGE

I can't imagine a more perfect marriage than tender, milk-fed veal and fresh sage. Speaking of marriages, we received news today that our old colleagues Aileen and Patrick Skegess have decided to separate. To be honest, the relationship lasted far longer than anyone would have predicted, especially given Patrick's predilections and Aileen's desperately brave struggle with alcoholism, but it's still a shock to think we'll no longer be seeing them as a couple at industry functions. As it turned out, he left her (apparently) but that's neither here nor there and I just hope that everyone gives them both the privacy they deserve.

4 VEAL ESCALOPES

2 TABLESPOONS LEMON JUICE

SALT

FRESHLY GROUND BLACK PEPPER

1 TABLESPOON CHOPPED FRESH SAGE LEAVES

4 SLICES PROSCIUTTO

KNOB OF BUTTER

3 TABLESPOONS DRY WHITE WINE

1. Place the veal escalopes between two sheets of cling film and pound with a meat mallet until very thin.

2. Transfer to a plate and sprinkle with lemon juice. Set aside for 30 minutes, spooning the juice over the escalopes occasionally. Pat dry with kitchen towel, season with salt and pepper and rub with half the sage.

3. Place a piece of prosciutto on each escalope and secure with a cocktail stick.

4. Melt the butter in a large, heavy-based frying pan. Add the remaining sage and cook over a low heat, stirring constantly, for 1 minute.

5. Add the escalopes and cook for 3–4 minutes on each side until golden brown. Pour in the wine and cook for a further 2 minutes.

6. Transfer the escalopes to a warmed serving dish and pour the pan juices over them.

7. Serve immediately, making sure to discard the cocktail sticks.

AUDREY'S TIP

If you don't have a meat mallet you can use any sort of blunt object. Often, I simply ask myself what the victim on last week's episode of *Inspector Wexford* was bludgeoned with, and use that.

15 July Colin Harris, the Art Director for this book, emailed today with some disappointing news. Due to 'cost overruns', several of the charcoal drawings Phillip has done for the introduction will now have to be omitted, along with his watercolours of Tuscan wildflowers. It would have been nice if they'd let us know this a little earlier, but I guess that's just the way things are done in the publishing world. (Imagine me walking into a restaurant and telling an executive chef that, due to cost overruns, she can no longer use fish!) I don't quite have the heart to tell poor Phillip yet. He has just discovered several old beehives at the rear of our property that we think might contain honey and is planning to harvest some tomorrow, so I might wait until then.

Tonight we ate the most wonderful *purea di verdure* (or 'vegetable purée', as we'd call it back home). Don't dishes sound so much better in Italian? If you ask me, they taste better too. Our meal was washed down with a few glasses of sangiovese that simply sang of Tuscany's rolling hills and terraced vineyards of luscious ripe grapes. So you can imagine our disappointment when Phillip read the label more closely and discovered the bottle actually came from Chile.

16 July Something of a 'dramatic' start to the day, with Phillip getting horribly stung while trying to extract honey from our hives. The poor love is not able to say much, as his face is still quite badly swollen, but apparently things went wrong when his 'smoker' (several lit Marlboro Lights) went out just as he was reaching for a rack of honeycomb, and the bees attacked. As I write, he's resting upstairs with a cool compress and a cup of tea.

Meanwhile, Helena and Ashley are relaxing by the pool. The two of them certainly seem to be getting on well, if the noise level coming from their bedroom each night is any sort of gauge. Honestly, it's quite embarrassing for Phillip having to lie there listening to his little sister in the throes of passion. Of course, it doesn't bother me, although I do feel that if she must cry out she could at least have the courtesy to do so in Italian.

'People hosting a dinner party
will often worry that their
guests are somehow "judging"
them, looking to find fault
with the meal or table settings.
This is, of course, exactly
what they are doing.'

17 July Helena and Ashley are both enjoying the relaxed pace of life here at Villa del Vecchio, not rising this morning until well after 10.30 am! We certainly don't expect our guests to dress for breakfast, although I did say to Phillip that shaving and some form of underclothing beneath a dressing gown would not seem too much to ask for.

We enjoyed a wonderful lunch today at the Pasquinis', who invited us all over for a family meal. Mariella produced a sumptuous feast of pasta followed by veal and several salads. Signor Pasquini was in fine form and had many tales to tell (or 're-tell', as by now we've heard most of them before).

What most impressed me was the way the Pasquinis' young grandchildren joined in the meal. This is typical of Italy. Here, children eat with the grown-ups, and they eat the same food. The notion of serving up separate meals of toasted cheese sandwiches or fish fingers is simply unheard of.

Italian children are also introduced to wine quite early. The very young will be given wine mixed with water but once they turn twelve or thirteen they are allowed to drink it undiluted. Anyone over the age of eighteen not drinking alcohol on a regular basis is viewed with suspicion.

When they were growing up, Phillip and I always encouraged our children to eat a wide range of foods. Each day they would be packed off to school with a lunch box containing smoked salmon and caperberry roulades or a mini compote of mushroom. This not only kept their tastes broad, but it forced them to develop valuable self-defence skills.

In Italy children are encouraged to join in meals.

'Italians love children and believe in keeping them involved in all activities. When it comes to cooking, rather than shooing them out of the kitchen I've always made a point of finding jobs for the little ones to do. You'd be amazed at what five-year-olds are capable of if given an apron and some properly sharpened knives.'

18 July For dinner tonight I felt like making something simple, so I decided to whip up some gnocchi with tomato sauce that we enjoyed out on the terrace with a chilled bottle of Elba Bianco and a loaf of crusty bread.

Earlier in the day, Helena had confided to her brother that she thought Ashley might be about to 'pop the question', and we honestly could not have provided a more romantic setting. Just to make sure, we left the two lovebirds alone for twenty minutes while we went inside to get dessert, but by the time we returned there was a distinctly frosty silence. Naturally, I didn't want to pry but I did manage to overhear a rather heated conversation between the two of them sometime later. It was hard to make out exactly what was being said (even with a glass pressed firmly to their wall), but from what I could gather the question that Ashley had 'popped' was something along the lines of, 'Do you think we need some time apart?' Mmm, poor Helena.

19 July As usual on a summer Sunday morning, the town is abuzz with bric-a-brac markets (be prepared to haggle) and people out enjoying the holiday atmosphere. Everywhere you look there are locals and tourists having coffee or checking out the shops while uniformed *polizia* move through the streets gaily handing out parking tickets.

Of course, religion still has a major influence on daily life here and hundreds of worshippers gather for Sunday mass at the cathedral. Once upon a time this event would have been marked by church bells, but the tower was damaged during a storm some years ago and the bells no longer work. Recently a restoration campaign was launched and each week we are urged to buy raffle tickets or auction items. The latest fundraising scheme involves a small group of local women who have offered to shave their legs in order to generate funds for this worthy cause.

Ashley left this afternoon. Phillip drove him to the railway station while Helena stayed behind to 'help me in the kitchen', code for lying on the couch flicking through magazines and sighing loudly.

GNOCCHI DI RICOTTA CON POMODORO

RICOTTA GNOCCHI WITH TOMATO SAUCE

Some people say that they find gnocchi a little 'stodgy'. They have obviously never eaten the homemade variety and should, therefore, refrain from commenting on things they quite clearly know *nothing* about. These gnocchi are as soft and pillowy as a freshly made bed.

250 G RICOTTA

250 G PECORINO ROMANO, FRESHLY GRATED

1 EGG

PINCH OF NUTMEG

SALT

1 CUP PLAIN FLOUR, PLUS EXTRA FOR DUSTING

EXTRA-VIRGIN OLIVE OIL

1 ONION, FINELY DICED

2 CLOVES GARLIC, FINELY CHOPPED

2 × 400 G CANS ITALIAN TOMATOES, JUICES RETAINED

1 BUNCH BASIL, LEAVES PICKED

PINCH OF SUGAR

FRESHLY GROUND BLACK PEPPER

FRESHLY GRATED PARMIGIANO REGGIANO, TO SERVE

1. In a large bowl, combine the ricotta, pecorino, egg, nutmeg, a pinch of salt and half the flour. Mix to create a dough then add the rest of the flour.

2. Roll out the mixture onto a lightly floured surface and shape into six tubes. Cut each tube into about 20 pieces, then press the tines of your fork into each piece to create the 'ribbing' effect typical of gnocchi.

3. To make the tomato sauce, heat a splash of olive oil in a frying pan and fry the onion and garlic until lightly cooked.

4. Add the tomatoes and bring to the boil, then turn down the heat and simmer for 30 minutes.

5. Pass the mixture through a food mill to remove the tomato seeds, then add the basil leaves and sugar. Season as necessary.

6. Bring a large pot of water to the boil and cook the gnocchi in batches. Remove each one as it rises to the surface, usually after about 2 minutes.

7. When all the gnocchi are cooked, top with the tomato sauce and serve with some grated Parmigiano Reggiano.

AUDREY'S TIP

It's a fact that some dishes taste best when eaten hot, so don't be frightened to encourage your guests to 'dig in' as soon as the meal is served. While robust conversation can be wonderful, there are times when it simply must be postponed. As for saying grace, I am all for giving praise to the Almighty, but not while a cauliflower sauce is threatening to congeal.

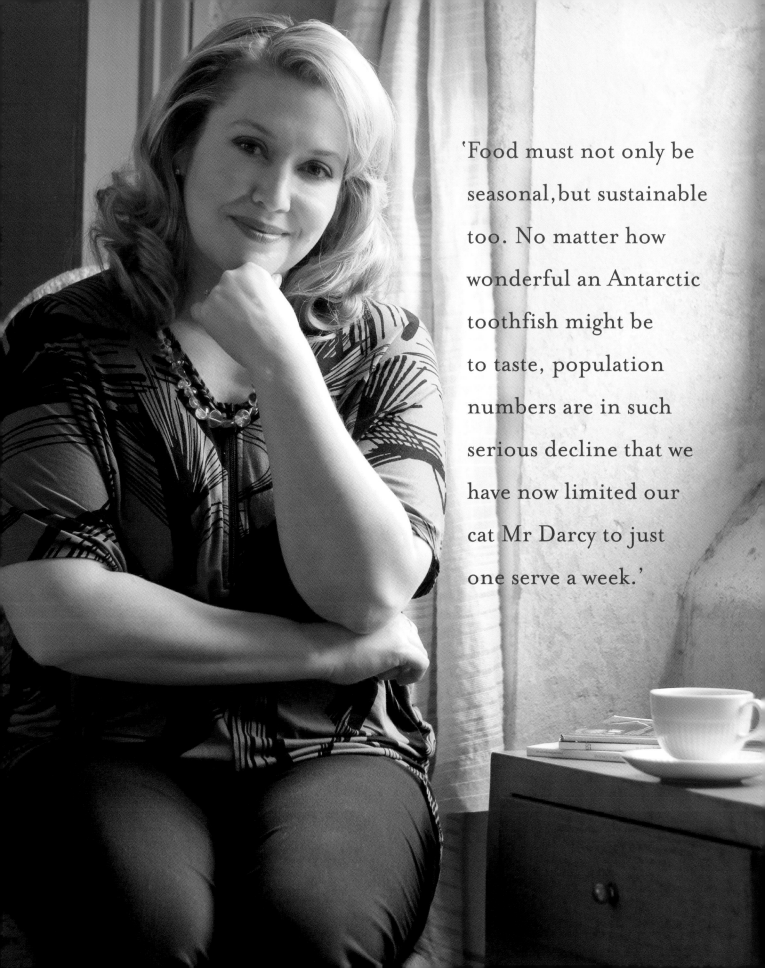

'Food must not only be seasonal, but sustainable too. No matter how wonderful an Antarctic toothfish might be to taste, population numbers are in such serious decline that we have now limited our cat Mr Darcy to just one serve a week.'

PASTA: AUDREY'S
TEN COMMANDMENTS*

1. The first rule, the importance of which cannot be overstated, is to use a LARGE pot. You have to laugh at people who think they can prepare perfect pasta in a small, shallow saucepan, not realizing that this will only result in a gluggy, unevenly-cooked mess which is no laughing matter indeed.

2. Do not start cooking the pasta until everything else is ready. I cannot stress this strongly enough. Cooked pasta must not, under any circumstances, be allowed to wait.

3. Never stop the cooking before it is done. Even if your guests phone ten minutes before they are due, in order to announce that they're 'running late', resist the temptation to turn the pot off or down. You'll simply have to start over again.

4. Don't even consider adding your pasta until the water has reached a vivacious boil, somewhere between lively and ebullient (but not raucous).

5. Actually, don't start again. Call your friends back and tell them not to bother coming. And then delete them from your phone and Facebook friends list.

6. After adding the pasta to the pot, stir it immediately so it doesn't stick.

7. The only way to be sure that pasta is cooked is to test for doneness. Remove a strand and break it open; a thin, white line in the centre indicates it is not yet ready. You are looking for a uniform translucent yellow, like a Monet iris, only not quite so vibrant. Another common method is to throw a piece of pasta against the kitchen wall. If it sticks, it's ready to serve. (If it falls to the ground you might look at getting the cleaners in a day or two early).

8. Drain the pasta when slightly underdone because it will continue to soften while you toss it. If it's already done then it's over-done so you might as well start again or give up and try something simpler.

9. Do NOT serve pasta with a pool of sauce resting on top. You may think it looks attractive but it's not; in fact, it's rather common.

10. Eat the pasta immediately. Have your plates warmed and drinks poured so nothing can delay the enjoyment of the meal. If anyone is rude enough to attempt to start a conversation, politely suggest that the discussion be deferred until everyone has had the opportunity to enjoy at least one or two mouthfuls and pass on their compliments.

* When this article was first published in my book Audrey's Boiling Point some of our more religious readers took offence at my use of the phrase '10 Commandments'. As I explained at the time, it was not my intention to be disrespectful towards God, Moses or anyone else involved in the publication of those holy edicts. And I'm quite sure that, had he thought of it, the good Lord would have happily added "Thou shalt not incorrectly cook pasta" to his list of forbidden practices, probably somewhere between murder and that one about the ass.

20 July Good news from home. The long-running court case I've been inadvertently dragged into has finally been settled. Honestly, I wish I'd never heard of Braun's BBQ Sauce with Honey, let alone lent my name to the advertising campaign. And even though the company did the right thing, issuing a voluntary recall the moment the first traces of contaminants (metal fragments) began showing up, the press had an absolute field day. So much has already been written about this event (pretty much all of it inaccurate) and I certainly don't intend to go into the details again on these pages. Suffice to say, having a range of food bearing your name wrenched off the shelves is a devastating experience and no one could have felt more upset than I, with the possible exception of the people hospitalised.

On a positive note, I'm pleased to say it turns out that the actual contamination did not take place in England, but at the manufacturing depot in Kowloon. That's certainly a relief, and to celebrate the end of this sorry chapter I decided some veal was in order.

21 July I received an email from my Art Director today, informing me that he's come up with a 'suitable compromise' regarding Phillip's watercolours. According to Mr Harris we can use them, but in BLACK AND WHITE! Can you believe it? What's the point? Tone and hue have always been one of the strongest features of Phillip's work. Honestly, you'd almost think they didn't want his artworks in the book at all.

This evening we were invited to dinner by our dear neighbours Vito and Theresa Strotelli. For me, any meal prepared by an authentic Tuscan housewife is a treat and this one proved particularly memorable. As special guests we were given the best seats – facing the window and upwind of Nonno Strotelli. Theresa served the most beautiful *antipasto* platter, followed by a white bean soup that was simply sublime (if just a touch over-salted).

I must say, the conviviality of the shared kitchen table is something I dearly love, as it reminds me greatly of my own childhood. At family gatherings we would often have up to a dozen people, sharing food and wine along with the pleasure of each other's company. There would be much singing in strong tenor voices (led by my grandmother) and general merriment. Special memories indeed.

VITELLA D'ALFONSO
VEAL ALFONSO

These hearty parcels take their name from Duke Alfonso, who, according to legend,
fell in love with a commoner, only to be refused permission to wed on the grounds
of class differences – and the fact that they were both men.

1. Preheat oven to 180°C.

2. To make the filling for the veal roast, heat the
   olive oil in a frying pan. Add the mushrooms
   and onion and sauté for 5 minutes.

3. Add the pork, garlic, parsley, sage, salt and
   pepper and cook for another 5 minutes. Remove
   from the heat before mixing in the breadcrumbs
   and leaving to cool.

4. Create a pocket in the roast and pat in
   the stuffing.

5. Tie shut with kitchen twine.

6. Heat the butter in a frying pan and fry the
   roast, together with the red onions, until golden.
   Remove and place in a casserole dish.

7. Add the flour to the pan and stir in well. Slowly
   add the white wine and bring to the boil.

8. Take the sauce off the heat, pass it through
   a sieve and pour over the veal and onions.

9. Place the casserole dish in the oven and cook
   for 20 minutes. Add the carrots and potatoes
   and cook for a further 55 minutes.

I KG VEAL ROAST

25 G BUTTER

3 RED ONIONS, HALVED

25 G FLOUR

500 ML WHITE WINE

6 SMALL CARROTS, PEELED

600 G NEW POTATOES, PEELED

FILLING

2 TABLESPOONS OLIVE OIL

100 G MUSHROOMS, CHOPPED

I RED ONION, DICED

60 G MINCED PORK

2 CLOVES GARLIC, CRUSHED,
   PEELED AND CHOPPED

I SMALL BUNCH FLAT-LEAF
   PARSLEY, CHOPPED

I SMALL BUNCH SAGE, LEAVES
   PICKED AND CHOPPED

SEA SALT

FRESHLY GROUND BLACK
   PEPPER

30 G BREADCRUMBS

KITCHEN TWINE

AUDREY'S TIP

The white wine sauce is based on a recipe
suggested by my editor. It's not particularly
original or even that tasty but I've included it
here to make her feel useful. (The truth is it's
a little sickly and you could easily omit it.)

More of Audrey's dinner party etiquette

Finger food

When serving messy food, such as prawns that need to be peeled, make sure you provide a finger bowl for your guests. This can be discreetly removed between courses and the contents used to form the basis of a light seafood bisque.

Conversation

In days gone by it was considered 'poor form' to discuss servants, sex or politics. These days the list of taboo topics has been greatly reduced, but there are still some socially no-go areas. Ill health, for example, is best avoided, especially if it involves gum disease or a colonoscopy. Similarly, marital disharmony is not an appropriate conversation topic unless the subjects are out of the room and you keep your voice down.

Oops!

No matter how careful you are in providing placemats and napkins, someone will always embarrass themselves by spilling a drink. While maintaining a fixed smile, make your displeasure known by insisting on cleaning it up immediately and with as much fuss as possible.

Seating

During a long dinner party I like to invite my guests to swap seats. This gives everyone an opportunity to share some time with me.

Setting the mood

For some people, good food, wine and conversation are sufficient dinner party entertainment. Others like to ruin the event with music. If you ask me, loud or intrusive music does little more than cut across conversations and conflict with people's ability to express their appreciation of your meal. If you must play music, make sure it is low in volume and light in style; classical piano or ambient flute tend to be suitable options. Anything involving explicit lyrics or percussion should be avoided.

Difficult guests

We all know the problem of the socially awkward guest, the sort of person who seems incapable of interacting with anyone else. A good host will keep an eye on such people and, where necessary, come up with small tasks that give them something to do, such as helping to serve drinks or taking platters around. In the case of profoundly shy guests, I find it's a good idea to give them a job out the back (such as washing glasses) to avoid any chance of them killing the mood by intermingling with others.

22 July As summer rolls on, we are growing as much as we can in the garden. The villa's excellent soil (enriched by decades of home pet burials) and warm climate no doubt help enormously. Even so, our humble veggie plots are nothing compared to those of our neighbours. Paolo came over this morning with a wheelbarrow full of fertiliser, teasing us by saying, 'You English cannot grow.' We'll soon see about that!

Helena continues to mope around the house. Phillip thinks she's depressed. I tried cheering her up with some freshly baked friands, at which point she informed me she is now allergic to pecans. To be honest, I found this a little hard to believe and so sneaked a small amount of finely chopped nuts into our luncheon pasta, just to check. Sure enough, no ill effects were reported so I suspect she's just seeking attention.

23 July Another festival day here in San Cisterno, this time celebrating the Blessed Virgin. As usual, festivities began with mass, after which several large statues of Mary were carried from the church and through town. We're told that this used to be a solemn, pious event but the influx of tourists has seen it turned into more of a raucous street parade. (There are even rumours that professional gamblers from Rome have been placing bets on which effigy will complete the trip first.)

Not wanting to miss out on the action, Phillip and I visited the cathedral, where we lit a candle and said a prayer. But when I got back to the house, Helena was still there.

This charming church is dedicated to Duke Lorenzo, a devout Catholic who, in 1364, refused to marry a wealthy contessa from Sicily until she agreed to convert – and shave her upper lip.

INSALATA CAPRESE
TOMATO SALAD WITH BUFFALO MOZZARELLA

The last few years have literally seen an explosion in tomato varieties. Red, yellow, grape, cherry – there's simply no end to the range now available. I read recently that horticulturists are working on a version that is white, very firm to bite and actually grows underground. It may technically be a potato. This simple salad pairs the freshest of red tomatoes with creamy, young buffalo-milk mozzarella.

3 LARGE, VERY RIPE TOMATOES,
   CUT INTO 5 MM SLICES
SEA SALT
PINCH OF SUGAR
400 G BUFFALO MOZZARELLA,* SLICED
6 TABLESPOONS EXTRA-VIRGIN OLIVE OIL
FRESHLY GROUND BLACK PEPPER
FRESH BASIL LEAVES, TO GARNISH

* Make sure your mozzarella is genuine. sadly, many so-called 'water buffalo' cheeses these days are made using the milk of cows who have simply been forced to stand in very damp fields.

1. Arrange the slices of tomato on a flat dish and sprinkle with salt and sugar. Allow to stand for 30 minutes before transferring to a decorative platter.

2. Place a slice of mozzarella on top of each slice of tomato. Drizzle with olive oil and season with salt and pepper.

3. Garnish with basil leaves before serving.

AUDREY'S TIP

I love to eat this salad with garlicky sourdough toast and a crisp white wine while curled up on the day bed leafing through back copies of *Country Life*. Bliss!

'There is simply no reason why children should not eat the same food as adults. My first meal was confit of onion in wine sauce. Although my mother was subsequently persuaded to start breastfeeding me, I believe this formative experience provided the foundation for a lifetime love of fine dining.'

24 July

Off to the nearby village of Pistoia for lunch today, where we had booked at the much-acclaimed restaurant Rusolata. And it certainly didn't disappoint. Chef Alberto Salano's ever-changing menu consists of *à la minute* creations that evolve, disappear and return in accordance with market availability, as well as his medication levels.

Shortly after we were seated there was a great deal of excitement when a local celebrity (who Phillip recognised from television) arrived and was shown to his table. The owner and staff were clearly in a complete tizz, falling over each other to impress their VIP patron.

This is something we used to frown upon strongly at audrey's. Whether actor, musician, politician or weekend weather presenter, I insisted our VIP guests be treated no differently from our non-entity clientele. Perhaps a complimentary cocktail or a few additional prawns in their *spaghetti marinara*, but nothing that could be considered 'fawning'. The only exception, of course, would be for royalty.

25 July

Helena left today. After dropping her at the station, Phillip and I decided to explore some of the pretty hill country to our east. After half an hour of driving down roads bordered with chestnut trees and pines, we came to a halt in a narrow lane where a young shepherd was herding his flock of sheep. Honestly, it was like a scene from hundreds of years ago and Phillip was naturally keen to take a photograph. Somehow, in the process, he managed to accidentally lean on the car horn, setting off a stampede that was both immediate and chaotic. We tried to get out and assist but by this time quite a few of the flock were entangled in a wire fence, while several others had gone over the edge of a small cliff, so we had no choice but to reverse hurriedly and exit the scene.

PROSCIUTTO CON MELONE CON SALSA VERDE
PROSCIUTTO-WRAPPED MELON WITH VINAIGRETTE

People often say to me, 'Audrey, I need something simple and fuss free for an appetizer.' And I think to myself, 'Do you really?' Personally I don't feel I've prepared a dish if it hasn't required me to be locked in the kitchen for at least half a day, physically ill with stress as each step is meticulously executed. And that's for a casual lunch. However, this classic Italian starter genuinely is straightforward and 99% fuss-free.

¹/₂ MEDIUM ROCKMELON

12 SLICES PROSCIUTTO

1 TABLESPOON RED WINE VINEGAR

¹/₄ CUP OLIVE OIL

¹/₂ CLOVE GARLIC, CRUSHED

¹/₄ TEASPOON SUGAR

1 TEASPOON FINELY CHOPPED FRESH
    FLAT-LEAF PARSLEY*

1 TEASPOON FINELY CHOPPED FRESH OREGANO

FRESHLY GROUND BLACK PEPPER

Sorry to sound unpatriotic, but flat leaf Italian parsley is so much more flavouresome than its frizzy-leafed English cousin. For what it's worth though, I do prefer our lard.

1. Chill the melon, cut it into halves and remove the seeds. Cut the melon into slices. Run your knife along the bottom of the flesh close to the rind, being careful not to remove the rind as leaving a small amount at the end of the slice makes for an appealing presentation. Drape two thin slices of prosciutto at an angle over each slice of melon, allowing some of the melon to show through the prosciutto. Now combine the remaining ingredients in a screw-top jar and shake well. Drizzle this vinaigrette over the rockmelon, grind a small amount of black pepper over top and serve chilled.

AUDREY'S TIP

Toothpicks can be used to hold the prosciutto in place but they should, of course, be removed before eating. On *no account* should these implements be used at the table for dental hygiene.

'Good balsamic vinegar is a joy indeed. Beware of cheap supermarket substitutes ('balsamic-style vinegar' is not fooling anyone) and avoid using any variety that has not been aged for at least twelve years. Yes, it may be expensive but personally I've always preferred to cut back on other luxuries such as new clothes or having the children inoculated, rather than forego the softly sweet viscosity of a good balsamic.'

26 July After having the house back to ourselves for barely twenty-four hours, our dear friends Ryan and Olivia Pestridge arrived today en route to Rome. They'd had a good trip, coming down from Zurich on the train, although one of Olivia's suitcases had apparently gone missing somewhere between here and Venice. 'Not to worry,' I thought, a tray of freshly made rice paper rolls would soon revive spirits and take their minds off this minor setback. Not so, it turned out, with Olivia spending the entire evening lamenting the loss of her precious bag and itemising its contents. Not even a bowl of cinnamon *zabaglione* could prompt a change of topic, and I was eventually forced to retire early with a headache (not entirely untrue). Still, it's lovely to see them.

27 July I'm pleased to say that everyone woke in a much better mood today. And with impossibly perfect blue skies framing a picture-postcard Tuscan backdrop, it's hard not to be happy!

After showing the Pestridges around town, we returned home for a light lunch of green beans with prosciutto and parmesan, which I served by the pool. Ryan and Olivia were so taken with this dish that they actually asked me for the recipe. I am, of course, well and truly used to this; at audrey's we would constantly be asked for the recipes to some of our more popular menu items. And, naturally, I always take it as a compliment. However, one has to understand that many of my recipes have been carefully devised over many years and I'm understandably reluctant to just give them away.

What I tend to do is give people the recipe but omit certain key ingredients or steps. Nothing critical, of course. If the instructions call for dried oregano, I might replace this with lemon juice. Or add twenty minutes to the recommended cooking time. Naturally, the resulting dish will still work, but taste slightly inferior to my original version, thus keeping everyone happy.

ROTOLO CON LA CARTA DI RISO
RICE PAPER ROLLS

Though not strictly Italian, these delicate rolls make a delightfully fresh and fragrant starter. Ingredients such as rice vinegar and Thai basil might once have been difficult to source in Europe, but Asian supermarkets are opening up everywhere these days and if you're prepared to overlook hygiene standards, along with obvious deficits in the customer service department (when I ask, 'Where's the lemongrass?' I expect something more than vague gesturing towards the back of the store), you should have little trouble finding everything you need.

100 G RICE VERMICELLI

1 TABLESPOON SOY SAUCE

1 BUNCH FRESH MINT, CHOPPED

1 BUNCH THAI BASIL, CHOPPED

1/2 CUCUMBER, SLICED INTO THIN STRIPS

6 SPRING ONIONS

12 RICE PANCAKES

SOY SAUCE, FOR DIPPING

CORIANDER FOR GARNISH

1. Soak and drain the vermicelli.

2. Place the vermicelli in a bowl with the rice vinegar and soy sauce and combine.

3. Add the chopped herbs, cucumber and spring onions and mix with your hands until everything is well combined.

4. Soak the rice pancakes according to the packet instructions, then lay each one on a tea towel or clean pillowslip to dry.

5. Spread a line of the noodle mixture down the middle of each pancake. Fold one end, then roll into a tight tube.

6. Serve with a dipping bowl of soy sauce and encourage everyone to 'dig in!'

AUDREY'S TIP

The problem with shared dishes is the tendency for some guests to take more than their fair share. I usually find a subtle comment, along the lines of, 'My, you're certainly enjoying that, aren't you, Ryan?' (or whoever), will generally alert the over-eager diner but sometimes it's necessary to be even more direct and move the serving platter out of reach. Only in extreme circumstances have I ever been forced to hide the cutlery.

'It doesn't matter whether I'm cooking for VIP guests at an exclusive degustation banquet or welfare recipients in a neighbourhood soup kitchen, I will always put in exactly the same level of care and attention to detail. The only thing I might consider reducing is the number of prawns.'

28 July

I have nothing but respect for restaurant reviewers, I honestly do. They perform a valuable role keeping the public informed, and, with one or two notable exceptions, they do this job well. That said, I do get upset with inaccurate or misleading criticism, especially when it is clearly motivated by petty point scoring.

Some years ago, a London-based newspaper critic (whose name I honestly can't remember) wrote that the service at audrey's was 'unacceptably slow'. Of course, I can laugh about it now but at the time it hurt us all deeply, especially the waitress responsible, who we were consequently forced to let go. What I personally found so offensive was the fact that this outrageous claim was simply missing the point. Restaurants such as ours were never about fast service. We deliberately set out to create a mood of unhurried elegance, a point obviously lost on Mr G. Neunhasen, whose complete lack of culinary credentials has since seen him transferred to the paper's television section.

I'm so glad we're no longer part of the restaurant scene. These days, the only 'reviews' I need to worry about are those of Phillip or my guests. And I can generally rely on them to be universally positive!

Olivia relaxes while I prepare lunch.

INSALATA DI VERDURA ARROSTO
ROAST VEGETABLE SALAD

Fresh vegetables, grilled and drenched in olive oil and balsamic, served with garlic and flat-leaf parsley, make a meal that will simply never go out of fashion. Unfortunately, the same could not be said of the wine Ryan and Olivia bought in town, a ghastly old Lambrusco that they suggested might 'complement the meal'. Naturally, Phillip made a great show of opening the bottle (complete with raffia covering!) before taking it into the kitchen, where he was able to discreetly replace the contents with a similar but somewhat superior vintage. Talk about a close call!

AUDREY'S TIP

Heat is the very essence of cooking. It's what causes individual ingredients to lower their barriers and intermingle with each other, eventually yielding to the moment, rather like vodka at a dinner party. That said, it's imperative that you use no more and no less heat than is needed. The last thing one wants is to startle the garlic or flummox your onion.

10 NEW POTATOES, HALVED

2 WHITE ONIONS, SLICED

2 LARGE CARROTS, CUT LARGE CHUNKS

4 CLOVES GARLIC, PEELED

1 ZUCCHINI, THICKLY SLICED

1 TEASPOON CHOPPED FRESH ROSEMARY

2 TEASPOONS CHOPPED FRESH THYME

OLIVE OIL

SALT

1 PUNNET CHERRY TOMATOES, HALVED

50 G PINE NUTS

150 G FLAT-LEAF PARSLEY, WASHED

2 TABLESPOONS BALSAMIC VINEGAR

1. Preheat oven to 200°C.

2. Place the potatoes in a saucepan of water and bring to the boil for 5 minutes until they're just turning soft but not cooked.

3. Put the potatoes in a large bowl, along with the sliced onion, carrot, garlic cloves and zucchini. Sprinkle with rosemary, thyme and a good slug of olive oil. Toss to coat the vegetables with the olive oil then season with salt to taste.

4. Spread the vegetables on an oiled baking tray and roast for about 35 minutes until they begin to brown around the edges.

5. Stir in the cherry tomatoes, and continue cooking for a further 15 minutes.

6. Toss the roast vegetables in a large bowl with the pine nuts, parsley and balsamic vinegar.

WHAT A PIG!

If there's a more important animal to the people of Tuscany than the humble pig, I'd be very surprised. *Pancetta, prosciutto, sopressata, musetto, guanciale* – all of these wonderful pork products pop up in a wide variety of dishes.

According to the history books, pigs were first introduced into isolated farming communities during the seventh century, providing a valuable addition to both diet and social life. They quickly became a staple part of the local food scene and were so highly prized that by 820 AD they had won the right to vote.

Every Tuscan family once raised a 'family pig' and many still keep one in their back garden,* along with a few chickens, ducks, rabbits and the occasional Romanian illegal immigrant. These home-reared pigs are generally female (their flesh is considered sweeter) and are spoiled and fattened on acorns, pumpkins, chestnuts and titbits from the family table. Many pampered porkers are even allowed to sleep inside on cold nights and will often be given the best seat in front of the television.

Then, during the middle of winter, this animal will be 'sacrificed' for the table. The day of slaughter is one of great joy for all concerned (with the obvious exception of the pig), and neighbours will gather from afar to help out, offer advice or simply enjoy the experience of having themselves splattered in blood. Just about every part of the pig is used and little is left to waste: the skin, blood, trotters, eyes, ears, even the tail and snout will find their way into a dish.

Porchetta is an entire roast pig that is often sold at local festivities and markets. The preparation and cooking of *porchetta* is a major task undertaken only by a specialised *porchettaio* (assassin). First the pig's organs are removed and it is washed, shaved and deboned. The animal is then killed, and its skin slashed. The cavity is filled with garlic, rosemary and plenty of salt, before the entire creature is roasted over a spit.

* Of course, this practice had to be banned during the 1990s when Porcine Flu broke out. It was initially confined to the animals themselves, but authorities were greatly alarmed when this devastating virus began spreading from pigs to their human owners (a particularly disturbing development, as the disease can only be transmitted sexually). Mercifully, the virus was eventually brought under control.

'Producing a great meal requires all of the senses:

taste, sight, smell, touch and emotion.

The only one you don't technically need is sound,

although I did once read about a study that proved

hearing-impaired cooks often struggle to make decent pastry.'

29 July For us, the communal table here at Villa del Vecchio is the central focus for the nourishing and nurturing elements that flow from sharing a meal. Seated around its rough-hewn edges with close friends, one can't help but feel it is a place of joy and an affirmation of all that is good in life. Which makes Ryan's insistence on telling inappropriate jokes last night all the more disappointing. Now I'm no prude, but I simply find stories about large-breasted nuns with unusually strong sexual drives to be in very poor taste indeed. Not only that, but they almost took our attention away from the arrival of this season's first figs.

30 July A somewhat dramatic day, with Phillip having to be rushed to hospital with chest pains! The poor darling had only just finished lunch, a wonderful dish of *risotto al gorgonzola*, when he felt a tightness in his chest. He bravely soldiered on through dessert (honey mascarpone), but by the time the cheese platter was being passed around he was looking decidedly wan.

    We rang an ambulance and soon found ourselves in the emergency room at Siena's Public Hospital. To cut a long story short, the doctors could find nothing wrong but Phillip has been ordered to take things easy for the next few days. As I write, he's enjoying a nice long bath and a glass of *prosecco*.

31 July

Phillip is definitely on the mend this morning, enjoying a hearty breakfast of bacon and eggs Florentine. He may even be up to a walk this afternoon, though we don't want to rush things.

Not such good news from home. It seems my recent article in *Wine 'n' Dine* magazine has prompted a veritable flood of angry letters. Apparently, my reference to diabetics as 'fussy eaters' has caused offence to some of their insulin-dependent readers. (Why these people are even *looking* at the magazine eludes me.) Anyway, we've agreed to make amends in the next edition by issuing an apology, along with a chance to win a set of measuring cups.

Dinner in town tonight at one of our favourite eateries, Casa Blanca. The food itself was excellent but the ambience was unfortunately destroyed by a group of diners at a nearby table who had insisted on bringing their two young children to dinner. One of them must have been teething and the other was clearly over-tired, judging by the almost constant crying that punctuated our meal. At one point Phillip suggested moving to another table, quite a reasonable request in my book, but this raucous group refused to budge. I actually felt sorry for the restaurant staff, who could clearly tell that the noise was disturbing other patrons but were powerless to do anything about it.

At audrey's we were committed to providing every guest with a unique and elegant dining experience, which is why we made the decision not to admit children under the age of eight including babies. Well, from the initial public outcry you'd think we'd just opened a twenty-four hour abortion clinic. There were letters to the local paper, petitions, even demonstrations (if you can call half a dozen saggy-chested stalwarts from the Association of Breastfeeding Mothers a 'demonstration'). But in the end we won the battle on behalf of our customers.

'Has the perfect puff pastry ever changed the course of world events? Perhaps not. Although I did once serve a celeriac and fennel tart to Prime Minister Tony Blair just a few days before he signed a major trade accord in Brussels.

I'll let you be the judge.'

Agosto
august

1 August

I love August. That scrummy, yummy, summer feeling when the days are stretched and the land basks in languorous heat. We're rising early to beat the crowds in town and get back home with our shopping.

Our meals are suitably simple. Today I served *bruschetta*, accompanied by a fig and walnut salad. The salad was simply dressed, which is more than can be said for Olivia, who has taken to sunbathing by our pool with little more than a brief bikini and plate of olives to protect her modesty. I know it's bothering Phillip, who has been out several times to check whether she needs sunscreen.

2 August

More sightseeing today, this time the nearby township of La Penza, famous for its impressive Roman amphitheatre. Phillip and the Pestridges decided it was a little too hot for exploring (preferring the shaded courtyard of a nearby café), so I found myself wandering alone amid the ancient columns, imagining the shuffle of sandal-clad feet, the swish of a tunic and the hot breath of a centurion as he grabs me roughly by the arm and flings me against a wall, his muscular arms pinning mine down. 'No! No!' I cry out, or would have done had a Canadian tour group not arrived to shatter the moment.

The La Penza amphitheatre.

The Pestridges have certainly enjoyed their stay here at Villa Del Vecchio and this afternoon they presented us with an Etruscan style vase they'd bought in town. They thought it might suit our hallway table. It won't, of course (the colour is wrong for a start), but naturally we put it there for now and thanked them dearly. I'll get Phillip to find a spot for it in the barn after they've gone.

PROSCIUTTO CON RUCOLA
PROSCIUTTO WITH ROCKET

This is a stunningly simple salad, but one that people still manage to get wrong. It's important that you carefully drape the prosciutto in casual folds on top of the dressed rocket. It should nestle elegantly upon the leaves and not – as I've seen it served in more than one 'reputable' restaurant – end up bunched in a congealed, meaty mass. I honestly wonder how some people think they can be part of the hospitality industry.

TWO HANDFULS ROCKET
JUICE OF I LEMON
EXTRA-VIRGIN OLIVE OIL
SALT
FRESHLY GROUND BLACK
   PEPPER
8 SLICES OF PROSCIUTTO
SHAVED PARMESAN

1. Arrange the rocket on a platter.

2. Mix the lemon juice and olive oil. Season with salt and pepper, then pour over the rocket leaves, tossing lightly to coat.

3. Top with slices of prosciutto and shaved parmesan.

AUDREY'S TIP

This dish can be extended by serving it with beans or bread if you suddenly find yourself having to feed extra mouths. Speaking of which, the Pestridges are still here, enjoying something of an extended break with us at Villa del Vecchio. Obviously, I haven't said anything to them directly, but Phillip is thinking of leaving a small note on their pillow.

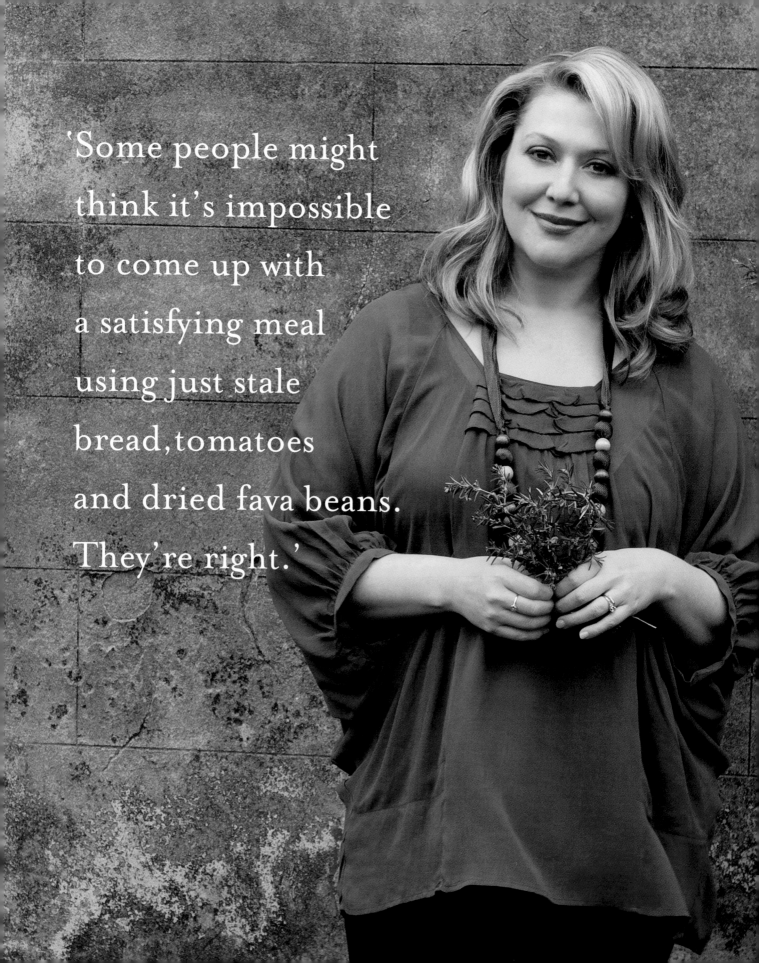

'Some people might think it's impossible to come up with a satisfying meal using just stale bread, tomatoes and dried fava beans. They're right.'

3 August   Paolo and Mariella dropped by today, just as I was about to serve lunch. Naturally, we had to invite them to stay and in no time they were tucking into a plate of *tagliatelle*. Look, I'm all for people enjoying their meals, but do they really have to make such excessive noise with the cutlery? Sitting across the table from Paolo is like listening to a jackhammer as he pursues errant pieces of food around his plate.

Late in the afternoon, Phillip and I went for a walk down the lane that runs behind our house. The sun was low and the fields were almost glowing with the most glorious light. We came across an old quince tree whose overhanging branches were laden with fruit. After picking a dozen or so, I just had to get back to the house and start cooking!

I simply loathe the idea of throwing anything away and will always try to make full use of every ingredient. If, for example, I am using egg whites to bake a meringue then I will set the yolks aside for a frittata or similar dish. Outer layers of onion removed to make a salad will be sliced and fried in my next pasta sauce. Tins or cartons of food dangerously past their use-by date can be dropped off at a local aged care facility.

COTOGNA AL FORNO CON MASCARPONE

SLOW-BAKED QUINCES WITH MASCARPONE

This recipe was a favourite of Gemma Knox, my sous chef for many years at audrey's. A talented cook and much-loved member of our team, Gemma was pretty much 'one of the family', and the day she left to get married and travel the world was a truly tearful occasion. The day she returned to open her own bistro diagonally opposite us was even less joyous and for the next 12 months we spoke only through our lawyers. (In the end we couldn't stop her but we did manage to force an undertaking that this new venture would not feature any of my recipes or bear a name beginning with an uncapitalized vowel).

750 ML WHITE WINE

250 ML WATER

400 G SUGAR

2 CINNAMON STICKS

2 BAY LEAVES, PLUS EXTRA TO GARNISH

2 CLOVES

2 STAR ANISE

4 QUINCES

200 G MASCARPONE

1. Preheat oven to 100°C.

2. Combine the wine, water, sugar and spices in a heatproof, ovenproof, lidded dish and bring to the boil, stirring until the sugar has dissolved.

3. Scrub the quinces. Peel (reserving the peelings) and cut in half lengthways.

4. Immediately add the quinces and peelings to the oven dish. Place in the oven to bake for 8 hours. Over this time the cooking liquor will develop a deep red colour and your entire home will be filled with the glorious smell of Christmas (unless you've had guests staying, in which case the scent of duty-free cologne may still be lingering).

5. Once the quinces are cooked, leave to cool. Strain and discard the spices and peelings.

6. Serve the quinces with their juice, a dollop of mascarpone and a bay leaf to garnish.

AUDREY'S TIP

If you don't have time to cook the quinces for eight hours because your guests will soon be arriving, quarter the fruit first, then combine equal quantities of sugar and water in a saucepan. While this mixture is simmering, phone your guests to let them know that dessert will be disappointing due to the shortcuts you have been elected to take.

4 August We've been charged with theft! According to the local *polizia*, we were witnessed 'stealing fruit from a nearby farm'. Honestly, these fools are yet to find the rogues responsible for breaking into our house or running off with our garden furniture, yet here they are prosecuting innocent people for picking a few quinces. Seems a little pointless, does it not? To make matters worse, there's been some disappointing news today from my publisher. Germany won't be doing a translation.

To cheer myself up, I've decided to roast some lamb. Not only is it one of our favourite dishes, but while the meat's in the oven I'll have a chance to fire off a suitable email regarding this appalling lack of editorial support.

5 August A quick trip to the market this morning to stock up on supplies. The bounty of summer fruit is quite overwhelming. I purchased an entire tray of luscious-looking avocados for just a few euros. Try doing that in Knightsbridge! I must say, we're really noticing an increase in tourist numbers. The streets of San Cisterno are jammed with camera-toting visitors and it's almost impossible to get a table at our favourite café, despite the fact that we are technically 'locals'.

One of the longest queues was outside Trevi, a new restaurant owned by one of Italy's most famous food identities, Romano 'Trevi' Boscelli. It's funny the way people flock to restaurants owned by famous faces such as Jamie Oliver or Rick Stein (or indeed Signor Boscelli), in the misguided hope that these 'celebrities' will be on hand to personally prepare each meal. In reality, such high-profile proprietors are often too busy promoting a new line of overpriced ovenware to come anywhere near their own establishments. Personally, I think this is wrong. To my way of thinking, all chefs should be obliged to visit a restaurant bearing their name at least once a year, even if it's just to inspect the kitchen and sack an apprentice.

More of Audrey's dinner party etiquette

Portion control

Serving sizes often cause headaches. One does not wish to appear 'miserly', nor overwhelm guests with huge portions. Where possible, I try to tailor amounts to individual diners. If someone is a big eater, I will naturally add an extra potato or two, or a few more slices of meat. If, on the other hand, a guest clearly needs to lose a few kilos, serving rice crackers in place of bread or perhaps chicken with its skin removed should hopefully send the message that you're thinking about their weight. (Sometimes I'll even avoid serving dessert to these people, knowing that such thoughtfulness will be gratefully appreciated.)

Self serve

For larger dinner party events it's often best for people to serve themselves from platters presented on a sideboard. We like to keep things casual and insist that everyone 'dig in' as soon as they are seated. Naturally, we don't mean it and have been dismayed over the years at the number of guests who blithely begin eating before Phillip and I are even *at the table!*

Table manners

When a course is finished it is customary to place the cutlery in the middle of your plate or bowl, an indication that you have had sufficient and are happy for the plate to be cleared. If you wish to rest your cutlery during a meal, lay it in a v-shape with the handles apart and resting over the sides of the plate. One piece of cutlery placed in the middle and one over the edge is considered an international signal of distress.

Place names

Place names are a wonderful aid in ensuring that guests are seated in the most appropriate positions. Some hosts insist on alternating 'boy-girl-boy-girl', while others prefer less structured arrangements. Those who are new to the area, or who are unknown to the other guests, are often best kept close to the host. Married couples, on the other hand, will generally appreciate being seated as far apart from each other as possible. Whether formally printed or handwritten, make sure you spell people's names correctly. If I glance down and see my host has written 'Audrie' instead of 'Audrey', how can I be sure she hasn't committed other such egregious errors in the kitchen? Has the meat been rested? Will there be eggshell in the soufflé? Has the gas been left on? At this point, I generally leave.

Plates

After the main course, plates should be cleared no more than two at a time. Stacking is both noisy and common.

Napkins

A word on napkins. I'm a cloth girl, always have been. Disposable serviettes are, to my way of thinking, abomination. You might as well put a roll of toilet tissue in the centre of the table and urge your guests to 'help themselves'.

PENNE CON SPINACI E RICOTTA
PASTA WITH SPINACH AND RICOTTA

From the day we introduced this dish at audrey's, it was a favourite with our diners. Interestingly enough, I tasted a remarkably similar version some months later at Margot Doeser's Hassar restaurant in Kent. Isn't it funny how some people think they can swap mascarpone for ricotta and then claim the resulting dish as an entirely new creation? Disappointing really, but remarkably common.

450 G PENNE OR SPAGHETTI

OLIVE OIL

2 TEASPOONS BUTTER

2 CLOVES GARLIC, SLICED

1/2 NUTMEG, FRESHLY GRATED

400 G FRESH SPINACH, WASHED
   THOROUGHLY AND FINELY SLICED

SEA SALT

FRESHLY GROUND BLACK PEPPER

200 ML DOUBLE CREAM

200 G FRESH RICOTTA
   (DEFINITELY *NOT* MASCARPONE)

2 HANDFULS FRESHLY GRATED PARMESAN

1. Bring a large pot of salted water to the boil. Add the pasta and cook until *al dente*.

2. Meanwhile, heat a drizzle of olive oil in a frying pan. Add the butter, garlic and nutmeg. When the butter has melted, add the spinach. After a few minutes it will have wilted down and you'll have wonderful, intensely flavoured spinach.

3. Season with salt and pepper, then add the cream, ricotta and a ladle of cooking water from the pasta. Let this come to a simmer, then season again.

4. Drain the pasta, then stir it into the spinach sauce. Add the parmesan, give the pasta a toss and serve.

AUDREY'S TIP

Some cooks are offended by guests who, having been served a plate of food, immediately cover it in a layer of salt and pepper. Personally, I feel no animosity for these people, just a profound sense of pity.

6 August

More bad news from my producer back in London. The commissioning editors at ITV have apparently decided to 'pass' on our new series, *Look What's Cooking*. It seems they've screened the pilot episode to a sample audience and it 'tested old', whatever that means. Honestly, aren't these people capable of making a simple decision without having to run it by five hundred mindless members of the general public? When I make a dish I don't send portions out to complete strangers asking, 'Is there enough salt?' I trust my own instincts, experience and skill. Now, I'm not suggesting that *LWC* (as it affectionately came to be known during production of the pilot) was ground-breaking television. And, yes, the eviction process – in which the bottom-ranked chef was pushed into a stylised cauldron of hot oil – clearly needed a tweak (the so-called Safety Officer we used was less than helpful). But given a decent budget, I truly believe it could have developed into an excellent series.

To take my mind off things, I decided to make some guacamole, only to discover that the entire tray of avocados I purchased yesterday are brown and unusable. I'm all for artisanal produce, but this is basically just fraud.

7 August

The glorious weather continues. If anything, it's a little too warm. I'm struggling to keep cool during the middle of the day and there's so much dust in the air (being thrown up by inconsiderate tourists' cars) that Phillip is finding it difficult to breathe. San Cisterno has been well and truly invaded by tour buses. It's such a pity to see picturesque squares clogged with coaches belching diesel fumes, when just a few weeks ago we had them to ourselves. There are so many people in town that yesterday we couldn't even get a seat at Mangero, despite being regulars. Not that you'd want to sit there, surrounded by Russian holidaymakers talking loudly into their mobile phones and ordering cappucinos with lunch (when everyone knows that this form of coffee is never drunk after 10 am). No, thank you.

'I like my salads to be conversational. I want the lettuce to really bond with the tomato, not just merely sit alongside it. They should be snuggling flirtatiously, saying, 'Let's make a go of this.' Meanwhile, the Spanish onion must be curled seductively around the olives, exchanging flavours like smouldering glances across a smoke-filled room. You simply can't expect to just toss everything into a bowl and hope the ingredients somehow get along. Lower the lights, put on some Enya and be prepared to use plenty of oil …'

BISTECCA ALLA FIORENTINA
FLORENTINE STEAK

These massive steaks are traditionally cooked over the hot coals from a red or evergreen oak. For us, this meant chopping up and then setting fire to Phillip's antique writing desk, but you might be able to find a more convenient source.

HOT COALS, IDEALLY HARDWOOD

THICK CHIANINA STEAKS,* BONE IN

SALT

Chianina are a breed of cattle that grow to a massive size as a result of careful breeding, although steroids are now often used by less scrupulous farmers. Be wary of any steak requiring more than two people to lift it.

1. Make sure your coals are hot and that the grill is well heated.

2. Place the steaks on the grill and sear them briefly to seal.

3. Reduce the heat by raising the grill a little. After a few minutes, turn the meat and salt the freshly grilled surface generously.

4. After another few minutes, turn the steaks again and salt. The important thing to note is that following the initial searing on a very high heat, the heat must remain constant and intense. If the coals even *look* like they're dying down, gently fan them back to life.

5. When done, the steak should still be rare on the inside.

AUDREY'S TIP

This amazing dish is often accompanied by a simple salad of chicory and bitter radicchio leaves, which many locals believe aids digestion. Mind you, Tuscans are also convinced that fennel can prevent HIV, so one should be a little wary of relying too heavily on medical folklore.

8 August Our culinary voyage of discovery continued this morning, as Phillip and I headed for the town of Montecchi for lunch at a restaurant called Carduno that had been highly recommended by friends. We're both adventurous eaters; however, there are some things we draw the line at. Today's menu offered *stracotto d'asino* (or donkey stew), a dish common in this region. Having grown up with these gentle, trusting animals, and even ridden them along the beachfront as a child, there was no way we could face seeing one on a plate so I settled instead for a simple dish of veal, while Phillip had *sfilacci* (shredded horsemeat) and a salad.

It doesn't take one long to realise that Tuscans will eat just about anything! Buristo (pig's blood salami), soprassata (cow's head, skin and tongue), picchiante (cow's lungs) and cibreo (chicken's heart, liver and cockscomb) all find their way onto the table. Yet, curiously, most people will draw the line at decaffeinated coffee.

'Of course, we have farmer's markets back home but these are nothing like the Tuscan variety. Buying vegetables from some jodhpured-Jenny who thinks she's a primary producer simply because her funds-manager husband bought an investment property in Oxfordshire is not quite my idea of an authentic rural experience.'

9 August

We were invited to dinner this evening by some neighbours who live several doors down from us. Giorgio and Maria Pantera were born in San Cisterno and have spent their entire lives here. Their two daughters, Marga and Domenica, both married men from the village and still live next door. Their son, Ettore, also married a man from the village and is currently spending time in a sanatorium near Florence.

Marga and Domenica prepare coffee

The Panteras' villa was beautifully decorated. Fresh flowers filled every room, adding a vibrant touch and (almost) managing to mask the smell of Tuzi, their elderly Maremma sheepdog.

Dinner was divine – *rotolo di vitello* (rolled veal) followed by a hazelnut semifreddo that I simply had to try for myself at home.

10 August

It's actually now too hot for us to go outside except first thing in the morning, so we're rising early to work in the garden and do the shopping. Then it's back to the cool of the villa, where I can cook, read and – most tiresomely of all – check on emails. Honestly, I don't know why people think they're doing me a service forwarding reviews of my television projects. Especially when these reviews are generally inaccurate, or motivated by petty point-scoring.

It seems Simon Bayley of the *Guardian* has claimed that my BBC travel series *Authentic Italy* has 'misled viewers' because a *few* scenes were shot in Croatia. How absurd. People watch my programmes (in great numbers, I might add) for the recipes and useful advice, not their GPS coordinates. Of course, I could respond but this only serves to give these critics an inflated sense of their own importance. I think I'll clean the fridge instead.

Good food does not have to be fussy. For breakfast this morning we shared a plate of freshly made whipped ricotta pancakes served with blueberries and cream, topped with a drizzle of truffled abbamele, (a honey and bee pollen reduction from Sardinia). What could be simpler?

SEMIFREDDO DI NOCCIOLO
HAZELNUT SEMIFREDDO

There's something about eggs, isn't there? The soft, yellow, bulgy, oily, bubbly belly of viscous loveliness that invites one to dive in and surrender to its very yolkiness. This recipe is made with egg whites only, so it's a little more austere, but nonetheless delicious.

1 CUP HAZELNUTS, BLANCHED,
   TOASTED AND COOLED
1 CUP SUGAR
500 ML CREAM
3/4 CUP EGG WHITES
1/4 TEASPOON PURE VANILLA EXTRACT

WARM GLOSSY CHOCOLATE SAUCE
80 G UNSWEETENED CHOCOLATE
200 G SEMISWEET CHOCOLATE
3/8 CUP LIGHT CORN SYRUP
125 ML HOT WATER

1. Grease a medium springform pan and line with baking parchment.

2. In a food processor, grind the hazelnuts and 3/4 cup sugar.

3. Whip the cream until fluffy and transfer to the refrigerator.

4. In a clean, dry bowl, whip the egg whites until soft peaks form. Add the vanilla extract and 1/4 cup sugar and continue whipping for around 30 seconds until glossy and stiff.

5. Fold into the whipped cream, then fold in the ground nut mixture.

6. Spoon into the springform pan, smooth the top and freeze for at least 4 hours or overnight.

7. To make the warm glossy chocolate sauce, combine the 2 chocolates over simmering water in the top half of a double boiler. Stir constantly until melted, then whisk in the corn syrup and water. Whisk until smooth and shiny.

8. When ready to eat, remove the baking parchment and serve frozen with the chocolate sauce.

AUDREY'S TIP

Serving this dessert with chocolate sauce is, of course, merely a suggestion. Feel free to try some other ideas of your own and see how far you get before realizing the foolishness of straying from my carefully composed recipe.

11 August

Mariella invited me over today to meet her sister Ana, who was visiting from Lucca. Spending time in the kitchen with these two remarkable women, both treasure troves of local cuisine, was an enormous privilege. Rabbit pie was on the menu and I watched in awe as they pummelled the dough with their strong hands, slapping it with enormous force around the marble slab before Ana produced a rolling pin from between her impressive breasts, and flattened the balls of dough into paper-thin circles. The rabbit was already in the pot (Mariella having wrung its neck earlier that morning) and in no time the most delicious aromas were wafting out of their ancient wood oven.

This, to me, is the essence of cooking. Women sharing their knowledge and love of food in a warm, nurturing environment. The sudden entrance of Signor Pasquini in his underpants somewhat shattered the moment but I'll value forever this simple exchange of culinary skills. And the opportunity to reproduce the recipe here.

Recently the plum tree in our back garden came into fruit and we've been enjoying a range of luscious deserts such as macerated plums, accompanied by plum ice-cream. Another night I made a delightfully light plum crumble. Breakfasts have been home-fired bread with plum jam, washed down with a large pot of steaming caffé latte. For dinner today we decided to eat out in order to sample some more local restaurants and give ourselves a break from the plums.

If your idea of salami is those pre-sliced waxy discs found on take-away pizzas then you only have to visit Signor Pasquini's underground cool-room to experience the real thing. Lovingly made from freshly ground pork meat, this fermented mixture is mixed with edible nitrates then stuffed into edible casings that are, in turn, treated with an edible mould to produce a sausage than can best be described in one word. Inedible.

TORTA DI CONIGLIO
RABBIT PIE

Italians love hunting, and Tuscans are no exception. Sadly, this has led to a drastic reduction in the numbers of local wildlife, with the wild rabbit population currently put at about twelve. Some of these poor creatures have been shot at so many times that they are in real danger of dying from lead poisoning. Luckily, commercially farmed rabbit is readily available.

60 G BUTTER

I TABLESPOON OLIVE OIL

I × 750 G OR I KG RABBIT, CUT INTO 6 PORTIONS, OR 6 READY-JOINTED PORTIONS

150 G STREAKY BACON, RIND REMOVED AND DICED

I LARGE ONION, CHOPPED

3 TABLESPOONS PLAIN FLOUR

750 ML DRY CIDER

250 G DRIED PRUNES

SALT

FRESHLY GROUND BLACK PEPPER

PASTRY

2 CUPS SELF-RAISING FLOUR, PLUS EXTRA FOR DUSTING

120 G BUTTER, CHILLED AND COARSELY GRATED

I TEASPOON FINELY GRATED LEMON RIND

2 TABLESPOONS CHOPPED FRESH PARSLEY

STRAINED JUICE OF $^1/_2$ LEMON

I EGG, BEATEN

2 TABLESPOONS MILK, TO GLAZE

1. Heat the butter and olive oil in a saucepan and fry the rabbit portions until golden brown, then transfer to a plate.

2. Add the bacon and fry gently. Add the onion and cook for 5 minutes. Stir in the flour and cook for 1 minute, then gradually stir in the cider.

3. Return the rabbit portions to the pan, add the prunes and season with salt and pepper. Bring to the boil, then reduce the heat, cover and simmer for 1 hour, or until the rabbit is very tender. Remove from the heat and allow to cool.

4. Preheat oven to 200°C.

5. To make the pastry, mix the flour with the grated butter, lemon rind and parsley and make a well in the centre. Add enough cold water to the lemon juice to make 180 ml liquid and stir in the beaten egg. Pour into the centre of the flour and mix to make a soft dough. Knead the dough on a lightly floured surface for 1 minute, or until smooth.

6. Transfer the cooled rabbit stew to a large, deep pie dish. Roll out the dough to an oval, 5 cm larger than the dish, and cut off a strip 2–3 cm wide from around the edge. Wet the edge of the pie dish and press the strip of dough firmly onto it. Brush the strip with milk, then cover the pie with the remaining dough. Press the pastry edges together well to seal, then trim off the excess dough and decorate the edge.

7. Make a hole in the centre of the pie to let the steam escape. Brush the top with milk to glaze, then bake in the centre of the oven for 45 minutes, or until the pastry is risen and golden brown. If the pie begins to brown too much, cover it loosely with a piece of foil.

AUDREY'S TIP

To ensure each portion of rabbit is tender, slice it lengthways and beat with a mallet as you would escalopes of veal, or an impertinent child.

12 August

One of the marvellous things about Tuscany is that you're never far from the sea, so today Phillip and I decided to head off for a few days on the coast. Cool ocean breezes would certainly be a welcome relief and the trip would also give me the chance to sample some of the region's excellent seafood.

We drove to Livorno, and from there south to the picturesque fishing village of Balzablanco, famous for its rocky white cliffs (from which the town gets its name) as well as its large tuna factory (from which it gets its distinctive odour).

Having checked into our hotel, we had time for a quick promenade along the foreshore, followed by dinner at one of Balzablanco's many beachside restaurants. Naturally, we ordered *cacciucco*, Tuscany's classic fish stew. Traditionally, this dish would be made up of whatever fish were in season, as well as the 'poor' (or cheaper) off-cuts often left unsold at the market. Unfortunately, our restaurant took this quest for 'authenticity' a little too far, all but omitting any trace of seafood. As a result we ended up paying 70 euros for a bowl of crab-flavoured onion and a few prawn tails. We'll be a little more selective tomorrow.

'Italians understand food. Their food culture is so much richer and more nurturing than ours. If they could only just learn to eat with their mouths closed.'

13 August

Can there be a more heavenly start to a day than a stroll along a pristine beach as the sun slowly crests the nearby hills? Phillip's doctor has suggested he do some regular exercise so the two of us 'power-walked' our way over the sand to the end of the harbour, where we stopped for pastries washed down with a steaming mug of hot coffee.

People-watching is a major pastime in the cafés here, and tables at the window naturally attract a surcharge. We find it's cheaper to take a seat in the back but be warned – patrons caught glancing out any of the front windows may find themselves slapped with a surcharge.

Dinner was at another delightful seaside establishment, where I was reminded yet again that the key to Tuscan food is simplicity. And when your basic ingredients are so fresh, there's really no need to do all that much to them. Phillip and I both ordered swordfish, which was simply brushed with oil, quickly grilled and served with a salad. Perfection! (Although it does rather beg the question how they could justify charging 80 euros for this and a few stale bread rolls.)

Each day, Stefano and his brothers head out seeking riches from the sea. In the past this was fish, but nowadays it's more often wallets and jewellery dropped overboard from pleasure boats that they retrieve and re-sell to their original owners.

The beach here at Balzablanco gets so crowded during summer that regular visitors have been known to bring their own sand.

SPAGHETTI ALL'ASTICE
SPAGHETTI WITH LOBSTER

We ate this simple pasta during our stay at Balzablanco, and it was simply divine.
Of course, lobster is considered an endangered species these days, so some Italian
chefs will use an alternative crustacean such as crab or rabbit.

1 × 1 KG LOBSTER

175 G DRIED SPAGHETTI

EXTRA-VIRGIN OLIVE OIL

2 CLOVES GARLIC, FINELY CHOPPED

1 SHALLOT, FINELY CHOPPED

1/2 MILD CHILLI, SEEDED AND THINLY SLICED

125 ML DRY WHITE WINE

1 TABLESPOON TOMATO PASTE

HANDFUL CHOPPED BASIL

SALT

FRESHLY GROUND BLACK PEPPER

1. Place the lobster in a large pot of boiling water and cook for 6 minutes. Remove and shock in iced water to stop the cooking process.

2. When cooled, remove the meat from the tail, claws and knuckles. Discard the shells and chop the lobster into bite-sized pieces.

3. Place the pasta in a pot of boiling water.

4. While the pasta is cooking, heat some olive oil in a frying pan and add the garlic, shallot and chilli. Sauté for about 3 minutes until soft.

5. Add the white wine and reduce to a third.

6. Add the tomato paste and half the basil and bring to a boil.

7. When the pasta is cooked, add the lobster to the sauce and heat through. Add the pasta and toss to coat. Season with salt and pepper.

8. Serve in a large bowl, drizzled with olive oil and sprinkled with the remaining basil.

AUDREY'S TIP

I generally find half a lobster per person is sufficient, but if not you could always add a little extra or try to find some less gluttonous friends.

14 August

It's hard to believe that our summer sojourn is almost over. The reality of this was brought home today when we returned to Villa del Vecchio, with a phone call from my publicist wanting to discuss launch plans for the book. Despite the fact that it's not even finished, there has apparently been quite a bit of interest (or 'pre-interest' as it's known in the trade) and I've already been asked by Waterstones to do some in-store signings.

Of course, I love doing book signings (or 'author events', as they're also known in the trade), but I do insist that these be properly organised and promoted. You wouldn't believe the number of times I've arrived at a store only to find a rickety plastic table, some half-used pens and a glass of (tap) water set up in the back corner next to the 'Men's Interest' magazine section. There's often little in the way of signage either, which makes you wonder how people are expected to even know that you're there. Naturally, I'm a professional and will simply do my best under the circumstances, especially for those wonderfully loyal fans who have made the effort to show up.

People really are priceless. Most are happy with a simple signature, but every now and then you get someone who wants a personalised inscription. I'm generally happy to oblige, provided it's not inflammatory or obscene. (I once had a gentlemen ask me to sign a copy of *Family Meals* for his wife with the words 'Now start cooking, b#$ch!' Naturally, I declined.)

Of course, my biggest concern with book signings is the tendency for some shops to insist on offering 'light refreshments' at their events. Not only does this risk coming across as somewhat 'needy', but there's also the added danger that my readers might think the rubbery wontons on offer were somehow produced by me.

Honestly, I could sign my name forever.

'After several months in Italy, I'm afraid to say our Italian remains pretty rusty. We had considered taking language lessons when we first arrived but, to be honest, so many people here in Tuscany are now bilingual that in the end it seemed rather unnecessary. On top of that, most locals appreciate the opportunity to practise their English so, in many ways, we're doing them a service by not learning their language.'

A CAREER IN THE KITCHEN

'How do I get started as a chef?'

This is a question I hear constantly from wide-eyed young food-lovers keen to break into the industry. But you know what? There's no simple answer. All I can say is that becoming a professional chef is not for the faint-hearted. It requires persistence, dedication, resilience, punctuality, courage, creativity, fine motor skills, discipline, poise, a willingness to work endless hours in hot, cramped conditions while wearing a hairnet, and sheer, bloody, single-minded determination. If you can't manage that, do not bother applying.

Then there's the ever-present challenge of dealing with head chefs renowned for their fiery tempers. Just about everyone in the industry has their own story of being yelled at, abused or 'bollocked', as it's more commonly referred to. Even I once had a soup bowl thrown at me by none other than Gordon Ramsay! (Interestingly, I wasn't actually working for him at the time, we'd just popped into his restaurant for a mid-week supper and I made the mistake of suggesting that the veal was under-cooked.)

But if you ask me (and you did), these sorts of experiences are an essential part of the learning process. It seems an age ago that I left college, just a fresh-faced young lass with a Diploma in Hotel Catering and Crowd Control tucked under one arm and a willingness to learn. In my first job I was abused, harangued, insulted, threatened, groped, locked in a cool room and almost branded with a skillet. And that was on day one. But I stuck it out and now, when I look back at my three years as sous chef at The Bloated Toad, I realise it gave me the grounding, the solid foundation upon which I was able to build my successful career.

I've got nothing against the current rash of so-called celebrity chefs. Some of them are quite entertaining and their love of cooking more than makes up for any obvious gaps in their knowledge. But nothing beats formal training in a working kitchen run by someone who truly knows and understands food. I'm proud to say that I've lost count of the number of great chefs I've been under.

15 August

There's never a dull moment here at Villa del Vecchio! Our neighbours Salvaza and Farinata Mazzinghi have been busy harvesting their olives, and they invited us over, along with several other friends, to help out with pressing the fruit.

It's an age-old process that involves sorting the olives and then pressing them in order to extract the oil. This is done using a heavy weight, traditionally a large stone or one of the Mazzinghis' two daughters. Of course, everyone has an opinion on the exact way to squeeze and process the oil, so there was much noise and laughter (not to mention red wine) as we all got involved. In the end we were all there for most of the day. It may seem like a lot of effort for just three and a half litres of oil but none of us would have it any other way.

Supper was provided by Nonna Mazzinghi. Like many Italian cooks, she refuses to use recipes, preferring to prepare dishes a occhio, or 'by eye'. While this works well in most instances, Nonna is almost blind and we were all served cannelloni stuffed with what appeared to be cotton wool. Still, provided it's authentic and accompanied by a crisp green salad, who could complain?

Tuscans take great pride in their olive oil and each batch produced is subjected to stringent quality control, with any bottles deemed inferior immediately destroyed or set aside for export to Asia.

'When choosing wine to go with a meal, I try to think of my guests. Will they be capable of appreciating the complexities of an expensive old-growth Bordeaux or would it be kinder to serve a more straightforward (but still perfectly acceptable) New Zealand sauvignon blanc?'

16 August

After a lazy start to the day, followed by a bit of pottering in the garden, we were forced inside to escape the heat. Phillip got stuck into some painting while I dealt with the usual emails from home. Among the standard requests for endorsements and assorted appearances was a letter asking whether I would contribute a recipe to a new anthology called *Great British Chefs*. Naturally, it's an honour to be considered for such a prestigious-sounding publication but I'm always wary about this sort of venture. When I release a book I have control over the contents, but being part of someone else's venture can be a risky move.

True story. I was once asked to contribute to a collection of recipes called *Mother Lode*. It was being put together as a fundraising project for Wooton Women's Hospital, and various high-profile chefs were invited to choose one recipe that their mother used to cook. So you can imagine my horror when the resulting book had my mother's Braised Beef and Leek Casserole sandwiched at the back in the *dessert section* without a proper photograph and the amount of cornmeal listed as '1 tbsp' instead of '1 tspn'. Naturally, when I pointed this out they were all very apologetic, explaining that it was a charity exercise and hoping I 'wouldn't mind', but I had no choice other than to insist on all ten thousand copies being pulped.

17 August

Well, the peace and solitude of Villa del Vecchio is soon to be shattered – in the nicest possible way – as Phillip and I welcome eight new guests to our humble home. Yes, I'm holding one of my famous Master Classes.

I used to stage these classes regularly but eventually had to stop when they became too popular; we simply couldn't deal with the demand, let alone the complaints from disgruntled applicants who had failed to secure a place. But late last year Phillip and I were invited to attend a rather exclusive charity event. To be honest, I can't remember exactly what we were raising money for but Prince Andrew was loosely involved so it must have been a worthy cause. And there was certainly an impressive guest list: dignitaries, diplomats, ex-Olympians. We found ourselves seated between a well-known newsreader and England's Young Amputee of the Year.

As part of the fundraising auction I was persuaded (after perhaps a few too many champagnes) to offer a group of eight lucky bidders the opportunity to attend one of my cooking Master Classes here in Tuscany. And tomorrow is the big day …

PINZIMONIO
RAW VEGETABLES DIPPED IN OLIVE OIL

Don't be put off by the apparent simplicity of this dish, as it's a colourful and tasty way to begin a meal. I've often served it at children's birthday parties: you can just imagine the looks on the faces of the little ones when – instead of brightly coloured sweets – you present them with a platter of raw vegetables.

2 CELERY HEARTS

I YELLOW CAPSICUM

I RED CAPSICUM

I RADICCHIO

I ZUCCHINI

I FENNEL BULBS

EXTRA-VIRGIN OLIVE OIL

SALT

FRESHLY GROUND BLACK PEPPER

1. Slice the zucchini and capsicums into long strips, tear radicchio into strips also.

2. Trim the celery, separate the stalks and slice thinly.

3. Clean the fennel, discard the outer leaves and slice slenderly.

4. Wash all the vegetables (and your hands if you haven't already done so) and arrange in a decorative bowl.

5. Pour the olive oil into individual bowls, add salt and pepper to taste and place in front of each diner.

6. Refuse to serve anything else until all the vegetables are eaten.

AUDREY'S TIP

This dish depends heavily on the freshness of your vegetables and the quality of the extra-virgin olive oil. The only time one should even *consider* using anything but extra-virgin olive oil is when you don't want its strong flavour to dominate a dish, or when you're serving it to guests for whom you have no particular regard.

'At the start of my cooking classes I'm often asked: "Audrey, what's the difference between stock and consommé?" And my response is the same each time: "Who sent you…?" '

MY MASTER CLASSES

Over the years, I have introduced so many people to the joys of cooking, from teenagers and university students to housewives and even old-age pensioners. They all arrive full of trepidation and nerves, convinced that cooking is somehow impossibly difficult, shrouded in complicated rules. Of course, by the end of our first session they all say the same thing: 'It's even harder than I thought.'

At times I need to be frank, sometimes brutally so. The fact is that people come to me with all sorts of preconceived opinions that often need to be challenged. If necessary, I'll get a student to heat the same pot of water again and again until he or she fully understands the difference between a rolling boil and a gentle simmer. Some complain and others even threaten to leave. But as I always say – if you can't stand the heat, get out of my kitchen!

Of course, there are always one or two 'bad apples' who insist on finding fault, making baseless complaints about the course. Some of these criticisms have been completely ludicrous. I never once insisted that class members refer to me as 'Madame' (although it would have been a nice gesture). And class sizes, while large, were always manageable; yes, forty students might seem a lot, but with the help of strategically placed mirrors and a decent PA system, I felt certain that everyone could follow my instructions.

18 August

In preparation for the arrival of our guests, I madly dashed around the house this morning, airing rooms, changing linen and putting a small sprig of lavender on everyone's pillow.

We'd hired a small mini-van and Phillip picked everybody up in town, arriving back at the villa just in time for welcome drinks in the courtyard. We then presented each class member with their own apron and cookbook and left them all to settle in.

They seemed a delightful group and everyone was in exceptionally high spirits, with the exception of a woman called Deborah who apparently doesn't cope well in hot weather. What's she doing here in Tuscany during mid-August might seem an obvious question, but naturally I didn't say anything and Phillip found her an umbrella. One can only hope her negative mood doesn't prove contagious.

Giving the class an opportunity to get to know me.

'To see the eager faces of my students, each about to embark upon an important culinary journey, I can't help but feel a curious sense of responsibility. Get it right, and I send them all home as accomplished cooks. Get it wrong, and they return to a life of uninspired meals served in a drab domestic setting.'

19 August

An early start today, as we have a lot to get through. Everyone seemed refreshed and ready to get started, although Fiona and Rachel were both complaining about hay fever, apparently brought on by the sprig of lavender I left on their pillows. Honestly, there's no pleasing some people.

I started the proceedings with an introductory talk, covering the essence of Tuscan cuisine, along with pool rules and which sections of the villa were off limits. I also identified which of my kitchen utensils were not to be touched under any circumstances. Then it was down to business!

Preparing a variety of stuffed pastas was our first challenge, giving me an excellent opportunity to assess everyone's level of ability. None of the group are professional chefs, although one woman, Louise Davers, runs a small B&B in Dorset and told me she is thinking of opening a restaurant there. Watching her prepare a simple *ravioli con la zucca*, all I can say is I wouldn't be booking a table anytime soon.

After a solid morning in the kitchen, we gave everyone the afternoon off to relax around the villa or perhaps take a nap. Meanwhile, I took the opportunity of an uncluttered kitchen to prepare a classic dinner.

TAGLIO DI VITELLO ALLA TOSCANA
TUSCAN VEAL CHOPS

When I opened my first restaurant, The Plover's Nest, with fellow chef Guy Dankston, we both had one goal in mind: to celebrate the love of good food and the pleasure of sharing it in a warm, nurturing and – above all – collaborative setting. Which made our acrimonious split twelve months later all the more upsetting. This recipe comes from those early, somewhat less fractious days.

2 × 150 G RIB OR LOIN VEAL CHOPS, BONE IN
$1/4$ TEASPOON FRESHLY GROUND BLACK PEPPER
1 LARGE CARROT, CUT INTO MATCHSTICKS
1 TOMATO, CUT INTO 8 WEDGES
125 G GREEN BEANS
1 SMALL RED ONION, THINLY SLICED
60 ML NON-FAT ITALIAN DRESSING
2 TABLESPOONS DRY WHITE WINE
COOKING SPRAY
1 TEASPOON CHOPPED FRESH ROSEMARY

1. Season the chops on both sides with the pepper. Place in a shallow dish with the carrot, tomato, green beans and onion.

2. Pour the dressing and wine into a jar with a tight-fitting lid and shake until mixed. Drizzle over the chops and vegetables, then toss to coat. Leave to stand at room temperature for 5 minutes.

3. Coat a non-stick ridged chargrill pan or barbecue grill rack with cooking spray. Set the grill pan over a medium heat or preheat the barbecue to medium. Cook the chops for about 7 minutes on each side for medium, or until cooked to your liking.

4. Meanwhile, coat a large non-stick frying pan with cooking spray. Transfer the vegetables and any liquid remaining in the dish to the frying pan, then sprinkle with rosemary. Sauté for about 6 minutes until the vegetables are just tender.

5. To serve, divide the vegetables evenly between two plates and top with a veal chop.

AUDREY'S TIP

I get so upset with people who refuse to take the time to allow meat to rest after it has finished cooking. Because that's just the point – it HASN'T finished cooking at all. After being removed from the oven, the meat's sinews and fibres need time to relax and release their stored juices. I've even seen one so-called 'celebrity chef' carve a roast chicken while it was *still in the oven!* It would be terribly unprofessional of me to name names, but needless to say N-g-lla was blissfully unaware.

20 August

There have been complaints about room allocations. Apparently, the smell of Phillip's paints gave Tanya and Raymond headaches last night. (Of course, the two and a half carafes of red wine they both polished off had nothing to do with it.) Anyway, we've agreed to do some re-shuffling.

Formalities began today with a very informative Powerpoint presentation from Phillip on the origins and history of Tuscan cuisine. Everyone found it absolutely fascinating, with the exception of Jarrod, who rudely left mid-sixteenth century in order to take an 'important' phone call. Well, it was his loss.

The aim of this morning's class was to prepare a three-course lunch, and I'm pleased to say that everybody rose to the challenge. Despite not having met before, the group has bonded extremely quickly and there was much laughter as we chopped, peeled, fried and baked away happily. The notable exception appears to be Deborah, who continues to come across as a little 'prickly'. It turns out she speaks quite fluent Italian and I suspect this gives her a somewhat misguided sense of superiority. I can assure you, there's a huge difference between being able to pronounce *mortadella* and being able to cook it.

Lunch was a triumph and everybody retired to their rooms in the afternoon for a much-needed siesta.

SFOGLIATELLI DI SPINACI E CARCIOFI

SPINACH AND ARTICHOKES IN PUFF PASTRY

When I included a recipe similar to this in one of my earlier books, a sharp-eyed reader wrote to tell me that artichokes did not originate, as I had stated, from Sicily but from northern Africa. I have always taken great delight in feedback from the public and appreciate helpful corrections, except of course when they are wrong. What 'M. Perrit from Worcester' failed to understand was that I had been referring to the globe artichoke, a member of the perennial thistle family known to have come from southern Italy, and not the more ancient purple-spined variety. So please think before you clog up my inbox with inaccurate and unsolicited submissions.

OLIVE OIL

I ONION, CHOPPED

I CLOVE GARLIC, CRUSHED

300 G BABY SPINACH LEAVES

4 ARTICHOKE HEARTS, SLICED

125 ML MAYONNAISE

1/2 CUP FRESHLY GRATED PARMESAN

SALT

FRESHLY GROUND BLACK PEPPER

PASTRY

I STICK BUTTER

250 ML WATER

PINCH OF SALT

I CUP FLOUR

2 EGGS

1. Preheat oven to 220°C.

2. Heat a splash of olive oil in a frying pan and lightly fry the onion and garlic until golden but not brown. Add the spinach leaves and artichoke hearts and combine over a low heat.

3. Remove from the heat and stir in the mayonnaise and parmesan. Season with salt and pepper, then set aside while you prepare the puff pastry.

4. Bring the butter, water and salt to a rolling boil.

5. In a separate bowl, pour in 1 cup of flour. Break in 1 egg at a time and beat well with a wooden spoon.

6. Combine the butter and flour mixtures.

7. Pipe through a pastry bag onto waxed sheets, making sure each 'puff' is separate and not touching another 'puff', or else they might cook together.

8. Bake in a preheated oven until puffed and golden.

9. Remove from the oven and spoon your spinach and artichoke mixture into each shell before returning them to the oven to cook for another 20 minutes.

AUDREY'S TIP

Anyone who has ever given birth will know the visceral, life-affirming outpouring of emotion where every nerve in your body is alive with the power of creation. That's how I feel about puff pastry.

21 August We took the group on a trip to the local market this morning, to help them select ingredients for tonight's 'grand banquet'. Then it was on to a charming vineyard estate owned by the noble Boluzzi family, where everyone was given the opportunity to sample some wine and buy a fridge magnet. On the way back home we stopped for an *aperitivo* followed by lunch at another village, before all climbing back onto the bus, which Phillip somehow managed to back into a fountain. (In his defence, he swore it wasn't there when we visited last month, although subsequent investigations proved it dated back to 1688.) Anyway, we all got home in one piece and it was straight into the kitchen for some serious cooking.

By now, I'd had a chance to assess everyone's strengths and was able to set them all tasks accordingly. Stephanie and Raymond are my two 'pastry chefs', turning out consistently good cakes and pie bases. Rebecca is most at home making pasta sauces, while the two lesbians, Tanya and Kate, have really taken to roasting meat. I've mainly confined Deborah to chopping and grating, a role she shows little enthusiasm for. Of course, I'm just trying to spare her the embarrassment of tackling more demanding duties.

'I love introducing new tastes and flavours to people who might not otherwise have experienced them before. At audrey's we'd occasionally get customers wandering in from the nearby council estate and, by the looks on their faces, I could tell they'd never sampled oysters or shiitake mushrooms before. For some, I'd say it was the first time they'd used cutlery.'

22 August We held a little 'graduation ceremony' this morning, at which everyone was presented with certificates, personally designed by Phillip, with each one bearing one of his magnificent watercolours. You could tell that everyone was pretty chuffed, except for Jarrod, who pointed out that his name was misspelled (honestly, there's no pleasing some people).

There's no doubt that every member of the group has gained enormously from the Master Class experience and we've enjoyed having them staying here with us. That said, I felt some of the comments left in our Visitors' Book could have been a little more effusive. 'Great time, thanks.' Really, Deborah? Is that the best you can come up with after four days of inspirational workshops?

Graduation day!

More of Audrey's dinner party etiquette

A word on table settings

Visual appeal is an important part of dining but it must not be allowed to intrude on or overwhelm the meal. Personally, I think one can overdo candles.

Oh dear…

We have all experienced the awkwardness and embarrassment of having a guest show the effects of too much alcohol. And the last thing anyone wants is to cause a scene, or further humiliate the inebriated person in front of his family, friends, parishioners or constituents. Try to distract them with a light-hearted comment or offer to call a taxi. If they do happen to collapse in the middle of the room, don't make a scene; simply throw a colourful rug or cloth over them and consider serving dessert on the patio.

Extra assistance

For an important dinner party, some people might consider bringing in caterers. To me, that's a little like hiring a prostitute to satisfy your husband's sexual needs. Not just morally wrong, but quite uneconomical in the longer term.

End of the evening

Getting people to leave at the end of a meal can be problematic, and a certain amount of tact is required. We usually find that most guests will take the hint if you begin yawning or blowing out candles. Failing that, it may be necessary to start the dishwasher. When your guests do finally announce that they must leave, don't make the mistake of pressing them to linger. Show them out, help them with their coats, tell them how much you've enjoyed their company and then deadlock the door.

Thank you notes

It takes very little time to pen a few words thanking your hosts for their hospitality. (And no – an email will not suffice!) Obviously, there is no need to go over the top. If the event was tedious or poorly planned, a simple 'thank you for inviting us' should send a suitably muted message.

23 August

After days of intensive cooking, it was time to give ourselves a break from the kitchen, so Phillip and I took a trip into town for a meal at Monatello. This popular restaurant is owned by Dario Monatello, one of Tuscany's most famous and award-winning chefs, whose photo adorns just about every wall in the place.

Personally, I have never felt comfortable about taking this sort of credit for a restaurant's success. If you ask me, everyone contributes to the dining experience, from the *maître d'* and head chef in his starched white apron through to the lowliest dish hand stuck out the back trying to unclog the grease arrestor. We're all part of a team.

Ego aside, it was an excellent meal served in elegant surrounds. Later in the evening we were entertained by a musical duo, *El Capitano et Tennillo*, who performed a series of what they called 'traditional Tuscan folk songs', although, as most of these were played on a combination of electric piano and drum machine, it was hard to fully appreciate their authenticity.

24 August

More beetling about today, with a car trip to the delightful hilltop village of Panzano, where we had a reservation for lunch. After a glass (or two!) of Santa Margherita Pinot Grigio from Orvieto, Phillip and I set off for a trek to the summit. The ancient walking path was indicated by painted stripes on the moss-covered rocks, and we felt like pilgrims as we made our way through the forest towards the crumbling walls. After a while the markers petered out and we were forced to navigate the final stretch using Google maps, somewhat detracting from the traditional experience. Despite the shade it was stiflingly hot and by the time we returned, Phillip was covered in perspiration. Only a large bottle of water followed by a decent serving of gelato was able to cool him down.

Some exciting news from back home. The LifeStyle Channel is apparently interested in 'moving ahead' with my proposed television series, *Out of the Frying Pan*. It's a brilliant idea, if I do say so myself. With six cooks competing to see who will be appointed executive chef, and who will end up as dishwasher, it combines drama, pathos, humour and paring knives. Fingers crossed!

TAGLIERINI CON MANZO E PEPERONCINI
CHILLI BEEF NOODLES

I must say, Italian TV certainly takes a little getting used to. On several nights Phillip and I have found ourselves watching a programme featuring large-breasted women cavorting in see-through bikinis while a short, moustachioed male host makes leering remarks. Such tacky displays might not be out of place on a game show, but this is the evening news. For such a food-loving country, there's surprisingly little in the way of cooking shows on television over here. I did, however, stumble across a programme called *Mangiare Presto!* (or 'Eat More Quickly') earlier in the week that featured this Asian-inspired dish.

1.5 LITRES VEGETABLE STOCK

6 THIN SLICES PEELED FRESH GINGER

1 LARGE RED CHILLI, HALVED LENGTHWAYS

1 BUNCH SPRING ONIONS, FINELY SLICED

1 SIRLOIN STEAK, TRIMMED

1 TABLESPOON SUNFLOWER OIL

250 G BUNDLE PAK CHOI, QUARTERED

300 G THIN EGG NOODLES

1. Place the stock, ginger, chilli and spring onions in a large saucepan and bring to the boil.

2. Meanwhile, heat a griddle pan until very hot and brush the steak with the oil. Cook the steak for 2 minutes each side for medium–rare. Transfer to a chopping board and leave to rest for 1 minute, then thinly slice.

3. Add the pak choi and noodles to the stock. Bring to the boil and simmer for 3 minutes until tender.

4. Ladle the stock, noodles and pak choi into large serving bowls and top with thin slices of steak.

AUDREY'S TIP

I know it's not exactly 'Tuscan' but every now and then one needs a bit of spice. That said, I've reduced the number of chillies – the original Asian recipe called for seventeen! Honestly, I'm amazed that these people ever manage to leave the lavatory, let alone get about on bicycles.

25 August Prepare yourselves for a shock, dear readers. I write today's entry not from our summer home in Tuscany, but from the cardiology ward of Great Ormond Street Hospital, London. That's right. We were rushed back here this morning after Phillip suffered a major heart attack (the doctors are calling it an 'infarction' but I really think that's just splitting hairs). It was during dinner last night. We had a reservation at Matteo's and I was just finishing off a sublime dish of veal (although, if I had to be really picky I felt the sage and oregano reduction had just a tad too much salt) when Phillip felt what he described as a 'tightening' in his chest. The poor darling didn't want to make a fuss and tried vainly to finish his *gnocchi al gorgonzola*, but I knew something was seriously amiss when he said no to the dessert menu.

A few hours later he was in serious distress and we made the decision to fly home immediately. The doctors have run a battery of tests and we're still waiting for the results, so it's naturally a very worrying time for us both. Instead of looking out the window at rolling vineyards baking in the golden sun, I'm staring at two Arabic orderlies smoking in a damp hospital car park. To make matters worse, dinner has just arrived and it's a plate of gelatinous grey meat smothered in packet gravy with a few over-boiled carrots. I can't believe Phillip is managing to eat it. A dramatic and disappointing end to an otherwise wonderful trip.

POSTSCRIPT

Can it really be more than three months since Phillip and I returned from our summer sojourn in Tuscany? How time has simply flown by. Since getting back we've both settled into normal life. Phillip's recovery is progressing well. He's walking each morning and, even though many of these trips end with an almond croissant at our local bakery, I feel the exercise is certainly doing him good. He's also been forced to modify his diet. Despite being a life-long salt lover, I am no longer letting him use it on his bacon and eggs each morning.

We have kept in touch with the Pasquinis. In fact, I received a lovely card and package from Mariella just last week, a wheel of *casu marzu*, or maggot-infested pecorino that apparently caused quite some consternation among the quarantine officers called in to fumigate it.

Work shows little sign of slowing up. I continue to be highly sought after as a food writer, corporate speaker and life coach. I've also been elected to the board of the northeast London Food and Wine society, quite a prestigious group although a somewhat fractious one. At our first general meeting last month six separate factional divisions emerged, something of a record given that there were only five delegates present.

On the television front it turns out that ITV have got word of our recent stay in Tuscany and are interested in the possibility of an eight-part series! They've already got a major sponsor lined up and are apparently very keen to move ahead. Personally, I'd be delighted with anything that highlighted the wonderful food of this region. And, even though budgetary constraints mean we won't be able to afford to film on location, I'm confident that we'll still be able to showcase the breadth and quality of Tuscany's regional produce within the confines of the Tesco deli section. So fingers crossed!

But enough of me and Phillip, let's talk about you. My sincere hope is that by reading this book and attempting some of the recipes, you have been inspired to step beyond your ordinary, pedestrian existence into a world of exotic culinary pleasure. I realise that not everyone has time to grow their own vegetables, or to only shop at farmers' markets for locally grown organic produce. And it is not my intention to make you feel guilty for not doing so (even if the food you serve is poisoning those you love, as well as contributing to the destruction of our planet). But we could all learn from the Tuscans who understand the importance of food. For them, eating is – almost literally – a matter of life and death. I'm an intensely spiritual person. I could quite easily be a Buddhist, if it weren't for the early starts and overcooked rice, and I truly believe that the mind, body and soul must all be nurtured if we are to grow. And, after a summer in Tuscany enjoying fine food and wine, I can honestly say that I have grown.

RECIPE INDEX

Regular readers will be familiar with the following symbols:

gf = gluten free

k = kosher

h = halal

lf = low fat

rd = reduced salt

However, none of them have been required for this book.